THE VIBRANT STILLNESS

Commentaries on Sri Lalita Divya Nāma
and Sri Dakṣiṇāmūrti Stotram

By Sri Yellamraju Srinivasa Rao

Translated, Edited, and Compiled By Padma Neppalli

NDIA • SINGAPORE • MALAYSI/

ISBN 979-8-89322-266-1

Contents

Acknowledgements *9*
Translation Notes *11*
Key to Transliteration *13*
Foreword *15*
Introduction *19*

The Secret Doctrine in Sri Lalita Divya Nāma

Translation Notes 27
Author's Preface 28
Sri Lalita Divya Nama 36
अवरोहण (Descent) 36
आरोहण (Ascent) 37

Chapter 1: The Descent **39**

1. śrī mātā 2. śri mahārājñī 3. śrīmat-siṃhāsanēśvarī 41
4. chidagni kuṇḍasambhūtā 43
5. chidēka rasarūpiṇī 44
6. apramēyā 44
7. svaprakāśā 46
8. sarvagā 47
9. sarvōpādhi vinirmuktā 48
10. mahāmāyā 50

11. mahāśakti 52
12. icchāśakti, jñānaśakti, kriyāśakti svarūpiṇī 53
13. citśakti-cētanārūpā 54
14. jaḍaśakti-jaḍātmikā 55
15. anēkakōṭi brahmāṇḍa jananī 57
16. ābrahma kīṭajananī 57
17. parā, pratyakchitī rūpā; 18. paśyantī, paradēvatā 58
19. madhyamā; 20. vaikharīrūpā 59
21. tattvādhikā - tattvamayī 60
22. charāchara jagannātha 62
23. sarvānullaṅghya śāsanā 63
24. pañchakṛtya parāyaṇā 63
25. sṛṣṭikartrī, brahmarūpā; 26. gōptrī, gōvindarūpiṇī; 27. saṃhāriṇī, rudrarūpā; 28. tirōdhānakarī, īśvarī; 29. sadāśivā, ānugrahadā 65
30. viśvarūpā, jāgariṇī; 31. svapantī, taijasātmikā; 32. suptā, prājñātmikā; 33. turyā, sarvāvasthā vivarjitā 67
34. bhavachakra pravartinī 69
35. sudhāsāgara madhyasthā; 36. kadamba vanavāsinī 70
37. kularūpiṇī 71
38. tvaksthā; 39. rudhira; 40. māṃsaniṣṭhā saṃsthitā'; 41. mēdōniṣṭhā; 42. asti saṃsthita; 43. majjāsaṃsthā; 44. śukla saṃsthitā 71
45. sumēru madhyaśṛṅgasthā 47. chintāmaṇi gṛhāntasthā 73
47. jñānavigrahā 48. ātmā 74
49. ābālagōpa viditā 75

50. manōrūpēkṣukōdaṇḍā; 51. pañchatanmātra sāyakā; 52. rāgasvarūpa pāśāḍhyā; 53. krōdhākārāṅkuśōjjvalā....76
54. sarvamōhinī....78

Summary *80*

Chapter 2: The Ascent **82**

1. avyāja karuṇāmūrti....84
2. dēvakāryasamudyatā....85
3. śivadūtī....85
4. gurumūrti....86
5. śāstrasārā....86
6. śivajñāna pradāyinī....88
7. paśupāśa vimōchanī; 8. muktidā....89
9. bahirmukha sudurlabhā; 10. antarmukha samārādhyā....91
11. mithyā jagadadhiṣṭhānā....92
12. vidyā'vidyā svarūpiṇī....93
13. duṣṭadūrā; 14. śiṣṭēṣṭā....94
15. saṃhṛtāśēṣa pāṣaṇḍā; 16. sadāchāra pravartikā....96
17. samayāchāra tatparā; 18. sampradāyēśvarī....98
19. mahāvidyā....101
20. brahmātmaikya svarūpiṇī; 21. tattvamartha svarūpiṇī....102
22. vimarṣarūpiṇī....104
23. parāpara; 24. prasiddhā....106
25. bhāvanāgamyā; 26. dhyānagamyā....108
27. dhyānadhyātṛ dhyēyarūpā....109

28. nirbhēdā; 29. bhēdanāśinī 110

30. nirmamā; 31. nirahaṅkārā 111

32. mṛtyumathanī; 33. nirbhavā 112

34. śāntā; 35. brāhmī; 36. parāniṣṭhā 113

37. hēyōpādēya varjitā 114

38. abhyāsātiśaya jñātā 115

39. maitryādi vāsanālabhyā 116

40. ajñānadhvānta dīpikā 118

41. jñānajñēya svarūpiṇī; 42. sāmarasya parāyaṇā 119

43. svasthā; 44. ēkākinī 120

45. duḥkhahantrī; 46. puruṣārthapradā 121

47. svargāpavargadā; 48. nirvāṇa sukhadāyinī 122

49. sadyaḥ prasādinī; 50. yajamāna svarūpiṇī 123

51. sarvāntaryāminī; 52. pūrṇā 125

53. śāśvatī; 54. śrī śivā 127

Summary *129*

Conclusion *130*

Hymn to Lord Dakṣiṇāmūrti

Author's Preface 139

Sri Dakṣiṇāmūrti Stotram 144

Meditation 147

Verse 1. The World Is a Reflection in Consciousness 148

Verse 2. World Manifests From ātmā Like a Seedling from a Seed 154

Verse 3. The Ever-Present "I Am" Awareness 159

Verse 4. Consciousness Illumines All 163

Verse 5. Misapprehensions about the Self............................169
Verse 6. Ignorance Eclipses Knowledge..............................174
Verse 7. Self is Immutable..179
Verse 8. Cause Manifests as the Effect................................183
Verse 9. Recognizing the Cause in the Effect.......................185
Verse 10. Sarvātmabhāva - the Fruit of Advaita Sadhana.....192

Conclusion 197

Acknowledgements

I bow in reverence to Sri Mata Amritanandamayi for initiating me on the path of the Divine Mother.

I bow in deep gratitude to Sri Yellamraju Srinivasa Rao for planting and nurturing the seeds of Advaita. I thank him for giving me the opportunity to transcribe and translate two of his most profound works into English for the benefit of the larger community of seekers across the world.

I thank Sri Sudhakar for making the original books of Sri Srinivasa Rao available and supporting me through the translation process.

I thank all the Swamis of the various Advaita organizations for making their online resources freely available for reference.

This book would not have been possible without the support of my dear friends and family.

I thank Dr. Ramesam Vemuri for his review of the commentary on Sri Dakṣiṇāmūrti Stotram, and for his infinite patience in answering my questions on the subject matter.

I thank Dr. Aravinda Rao Karanam for his valuable review feedback on the book and for the Foreword he so graciously provided on my request.

I also thank my dear friend Sri Ravi Thotapalli for his copyedits on the commentary on Sri Lalita Divya Nāma.

I thank my elderly mother Subhadra Patibanda for her patience and support while I was preoccupied with the book. I also thank my husband Prabhakar Neppalli, my brother Sivakumar Patibanda, and my daughter Vidya Spandana for their active involvement in helping me get the manuscript ready for publication.

In spite of all the help I received from friends and family, if any errors have crept into this book (which I am sure they did!), those are entirely mine.

Last but not the least, I thank Sri G. S. Prakash, the artist in South India, for the artwork he provided for the front cover of this book. Inspired by the contents of the book, Sri Prakash painted in the vibrancy of Shakti and the stillness of Shiva into this painting, which he aptly named Hidden Divinity. Hidden Divinity is full of symbolism for an intuitive eye to discern and rejoice in.

Translation Notes

This English version of the two texts originally written by Sri Srinivasa Rao in Telugu is an interpretative translation. This book targets mature seekers who are familiar with the basic concepts and terminology of Advaita Vedanta.

To throw a bridge across the barrier of language, I had to make some painful, but conscientious decisions to slightly drift from the narrative Telugu idiom and style of Sri Srinivasa Rao. I occasionally reworded some sentences for conciseness, added an extra word or a sentence here and there to remove ambiguity, and slightly rearranged some paragraphs to improve the overall flow. I have, however, taken extreme care to make sure none of the changes I made violate the core teaching that Sri Srinivasa Rao so lucidly brings forth in his commentary.

If any errors have inadvertently crept into the translation, I offer my sincere apologies. These errors are entirely my responsibility and may not be attributed to Sri Yellamraju Srinivas Rao or his original Telugu text.

In this translation, Goddess Lalitha has been variously referred to as śakti, Goddess, Devī, Divine Mother, Supreme Power, Supreme Consciousness, etc., and Lord Dakṣiṇāmūrti has been referred to as śiva, brahman, Self, Supreme Consciousness, Universal Consciousness, etc.

The transliteration of Sanskrit verses or mantras are italicized so that they appear distinct and are not lost within the body text, but other Sanskrit transliterated words are presented in regular font to minimize distraction.

A glossary has not been provided because Sanskrit terms have been defined right in the context where they appear within the text.

I hope I have succeeded in presenting an inspiring and joyful reading of Sri Srinivasa Rao's insightful commentaries on the glory of the One that manifests as many.

– Padma Neppalli
Fremont, CA, US
Feb 2024

Key to Transliteration

The International Alphabet for Sanskrit Transliteration (IAST) has been used to transliterate Sanskrit words. The table below provides a key to the pronunciation of some Sanskrit letters. For an exhaustive list or additional help in pronouncing the Sanskrit words in this book, please refer to other sources.

Letters	**Sound Like**	**Sanskrit Examples**
a	o in come	amsa
ā	a in calm	ātmā
i	i in gift	asti
ī	ee in feel	īśvara
u	u in full	upādhi
ū	oo in spoon	pūrṇa
ai	ai in tail	dvaita
c	ch in **ch**urch	cit, sancita, chāndogya
da	da in **th**en	dama, nididhyāsana
ṇ	n in u*n*der	prāṇa, pramāṇa
s	s in **S**un	sandhyā
ś	s in *s*at	śravaṇa
ṣ	sh in **sh**ut	ṣoḍaśa
ṭa	t in **t**ouch	karta, nitya
th	th in anthill	anuṣṭhāna
jna	hard gya in English	jñāna

Note: The letter "s" is added to the end of the Sanskrit terms to indicate plural. The letter 's' is preceded by a hyphen (-) to avoid confusion as being part of the Sanskrit word.

Foreword

It is a matter of great delight to see the works of Sri Yellamraju Srinivasa Rao getting translated into English. I had the good fortune of having known him for more than thirty years and heard some of his talks on various subjects relating to Vedanta. Sri Yellamraju had covered almost all seminal texts of Vedanta, taught them, and wrote on them. He also wrote critical essays on the two great epics the *Ramayana* and the *Mahabharata* and on *Srimad Bhagavatam*. He is a no-nonsense teacher, who drives home the essentials of non-dual philosophy with force and conviction. At first, a student may be amazed by his bold statements which sometimes appear radical. A senior student will realize that older writers like Sage Vidyaranya had also used the same no-nonsense language in treatises like *Vedanta Panchadasi*.

Smt. Padma Neppalli is true student of a great master, in the sense that she is not content with mere reading, but she is bringing out the works of her guru to a global audience in English. She has done long years of sravanam, listening to a competent guru and understanding the subject, followed by mananam, logical validation of what is learnt, and she is now in the next step called nididhyasanam, internalizing the teaching of Vedanta. She is shaping herself as a teacher to carry on the torch of Vedanta.

The books of Sri Yellamraju are quite often brief, giving the essence of the text he takes up. Two such texts are contained in this small volume. One relates to the inner meaning of the names of Lalita and the other relates to Shankaracharya's text on Dakṣiṇāmūrti, who is called the *jnana-avatar* of Shiva. Both are the most revered texts in Vedantic literature.

In the first book Sri Yellamraju has taken the liberty of selecting 108 names from out of the thousand names of Lalita and of arranging them in such a way that they form a capsule course for a seeker. The first 54 names describe the descent of human being, the individual *jīva* getting entangled in the cycle of birth and death (called samsara). The next 54 names describe the ascent, describing the way to get released from this cycle by realizing oneness with the Supreme Reality. This is the famous paradigm of *adhyāropa* (superimposition of a false identity) and *apavāda* (getting rid of that identity). Thus, the book follows the tradition established by traditional masters.

It is good that in her foreword the translator made it clear that the book is for a reader who is already having some acquaintance with the terminology of Vedanta. Even this is an understatement, because the books taken up by her are among the serious passages in Vedanta. The names of Lalita appear very simple at the primary level, making her appear like some goddess in the middle of the ocean. The real meaning, however, is different. For instance, the name, *raho-yāga-kramārādhyā,* literally means that the goddess can be known by esoteric yagna. It can be mistaken for a tantric way of yagna, *vāmācāra*, which is disapproved by great acharyas. The word *rahas* means solitude, which means that the seeker has to contemplate Reality without any disturbance. The process is called *jñāna yajña.* In another name, the goddess is said to hold the sugarcane as bow and the five senses as arrows. The mind is the sugarcane bow, as it is the source of all pleasures. The more we take, the more desirable they appear, as in the sugarcane. The five elements, earth, water, fire, air and space, manifest as the five sense organs we have. These sense organs shoot out to sense objects like arrows and desire them.

Why do the old texts use such symbolic expressions? The Upanishads say that gods take delight when they are referred to in an esoteric language, *parokṣa-priyā iva hi devāḥ.* The lay reader is content with the primary meaning of the word, but a serious student investigates the figurative or symbolic meaning. Sri Yellamraju explained most words by giving the etymological and suggested meanings in most cases and the translator has taken great care to explain them in English.

The second book *Dakṣiṇāmūrti Stotram* is as mysterious as the earlier one. It is not a hymn to a god with name and form, but it is the very essence of self-knowledge. The Supreme Reality, defined in the Upanishads as infinitely existing consciousness, is the only entity pervading the universe, manifesting as sentient and insentient. It is the same entity present in the guru and in the seeker. The apparent distinction between the cosmic being Iśvara, guru and the self, disappears on proper investigation into the nature of self, and the seeker realizes his real self as non-dual Brahman. In this too, Sri Yellamraju has excelled in capturing the essence of the highest concepts of Vedanta in as simple terms as possible. He appears rather unkind to ritualist worship, but that is what Vedanta expects from a seeker at a higher level.

The outcome of the study of Vedanta, as Sri Yellamraju writes in his epilogue to the *Stotram*, is to attain *sarvātmabhāva*, the experience of the self in all beings, a very egalitarian idea which is unique to Upanishadic thought.

One must congratulate the translator for having presented such complex texts in a lucid style to the enlightened audience of the west.

– Dr. K. Aravinda Rao

Retired DGP, currently teaching at the Advaita Academy

Introduction

Who am I? What is this world I see? What is my relationship to it? People have pondered these questions for ages. Awed by the power of nature and their complete dependence on it, they struggled to find ways to overcome its challenges. Claiming lordship over all creatures, land, and resources, some tried to control and subdue it. Helpless and humbled by its invincible power, others worshiped and lived in harmony with it. Cultures around the world developed around these beliefs. Belief-systems later evolved into ideologies and religions.

Thousands of years ago, isolated by the Himalayas on one side and the oceans on three sides, the people of Bharat (India) discerned and developed their own unique philosophy and way of life called *sanātana dharma* (eternal wisdom), later known as Hinduism. *Sanātana dharma* stands on three scriptural pillars of knowledge: the Vedas, Puranas, and the two epics, Ramayana and Mahabharata. Considered timeless, impersonal, and authorless, the four Vedas are broadly divided into two portions each: karma kāṇḍa and jñāna kāṇḍa. Karma kāṇḍa is replete with mantras, benedictions, rituals, ceremonies, and sacrifices to appease the various forces of nature for the well-being of the individual and the community. Jñāna kāṇḍa, also known as Vedanta (end of Vedas), contains the Upanishads, which deal with meditation, philosophy, consciousness, and ontological knowledge. Puranas are mythologies eulogizing various deities of the Hindu pantheon. They are an artistic and engaging expression of the Vedas made more accessible to common man.

Ingrained in *sanātana dharma*, India gave birth to many great seers, religions, and philosophies. Awed by the incredible and transient universe around them, sages of India contemplated on the unchanging reality behind the changing visage. Several philosophies and practices, such as yoga, upāsanā (ritual), and jñāna (Knowledge) evolved from their contemplations. Advaita (Non-Duality), however, stands out as the sublime knowledge. Advaita, the essence of the Upanishads, asserts that brahman - Formless, Infinite, Immutable Existence-Consciousness-Bliss (*sat-cit-ānanda*) - is the only Reality, and everything else is a mere appearance. Over several hundreds of years, different flavors of Advaita thought emerged. Of these flavors that later developed into complete non-dual doctrines, Advaita Vedanta of Adi Shankarācārya in the 8th century, Shaiva Advaita of Abhinavagupta in the 10th century, and Viśiṣṭādvaita (qualified non-duality) of Ramanuja in the 12th century are the most prominent. Since this book is a blend of the non-dual teachings of both Shaiva Advaita and Advaita Vedanta, a closer look at these two traditions could be helpful.

Advaita Vedanta is a non-dualistic branch of Vedanta. Gaudapada was among its earliest Advaita gurus, followed by Govindapada and Shankara Bhagavadpada. Shankara Bhagavadpada synthesized and systematized Advaita knowledge and developed it into a complete doctrine, the core of which is the liberating knowledge of the Self. He wrote elaborate commentaries on the Upanishads, Brahma Sutras, and Bhagavad Gita, and several treatises and hymns, such as Aparokshanubhuti and Dakṣiṇāmūrti Stotra.

Shaiva Advaita (Kashmir Shaivism) is a branch of Tantra, an esoteric and philosophical tradition of India. This tantric tradition reached its highest form of sophistication in 1000 AD under the great mystic and philosopher Abhinavagupta. Some of the most profound and brilliant works of this tradition are Abhinavagupta's Tantraloka (Elucidation of Tantra) and Kshemeraja's Pratyabhigna Hridayam (The Secret of Self Recognition).

Advaita Vedanta and Shaiva Advaita are similar in some ways and differ in other ways. They agree on the ultimate non-dual absolute reality and explicate on the relation between the absolute reality and the relative world. Vedanta is a top-down approach to truth. It begins in the plane of Intuition and flows downwards. Whereas, Tantra is a bottom-up approach. It begins from the material plane and flows upwards to truth. They both agree that mukti (liberation from the cycle of birth and death) is the ultimate goal of human life. While they concur on the basic tenets, they differ in the means for attaining the ultimate goal. Advaita Vedanta draws a distinction between the Absolute Reality of brahman and the relative reality of the phenomenal world. While declaring that brahman alone is Real, Advaita Vedanta asserts that the phenomenal world perceived by the senses is mithya, a seemingly real appearance. Shaiva Advaita, on the other hand, asserts that the phenomenal world is real as the manifestation of the immanent power (*śakti*) of *parama śiva* (*Universal* Consciousness or *brahman*). Power is not different from the Powerful One. *Śakti* is not different from *parama śiva.*

Sri Yellamraju Srinivasa Rao was a staunch non-dualist and proponent of Advaita Vedanta. While he expounded tirelessly on Shankara's Advaita Vedanta, he was also well read and accomplished in other non-dual traditions. His penetrating vision could grasp, assimilate, and reconcile the common threads and apparent differences in each tradition. He drank freely from the cup of Shaiva Advaita, Buddhism, and Sufism and shared the nectar of Advaita from each tradition with his students to reinforce lofty concepts or to open their hearts to the mystical experience of "that" which is beyond the mind and senses. Charged with the spirit of Advaita, his talks were ever fresh and inspiring, even when he was expounding on the most intellectually challenging non-dual concepts.

Sri Srinivasa Rao had as much reverence for Abhinavagupta as he did for Shankara. In his introductory discourse on Tripura Rahasyam, Sri Srinivasa Rao says, "Advaita is the Absolute Truth. This is the premise of both Shaiva Advaita and Shankara Advaita. Although these two traditions are referred to with different names, the names are synonymous. Shaiva Advaita refers to the Universal Consciousness as *śivam*, Shankara Advaita refers to it as *brahman*."

In his talks and writings, Sri Srinivasa Rao's unflinching focus was on *brahma vidya*, the knowledge of brahman. In strong and compelling words, he repeatedly warned his students not to succumb to old tendencies and the lure of kāmyā karmas (desire-based actions), and to stay committed to the path of Advaita. Firm commitment to the truth and conviction in the teaching, he insisted, will bear fruit in this very life-time. Not only did he brilliantly expound the Advaita doctrine, he also suggested ways to practice it. In his talk on Advaita Darsana (Non-Dual Vision), for instance, he takes his audience step-by-step through the process of contemplation and meditation (manana and nididhyāsana) and concludes with a sweeping statement that there are only two ways one can realize the truth: either by grasping *brahman* directly through Self-Knowledge (removing ignorance) or, if one is not capable of doing so, by meditating on *brahman* as the absolute reality of everything. The former is a direct path to liberation and the latter is indirect.

This book is a translation and compilation of two books written by Sri Srinivasa Rao. The first is a commentary on 108 names or mantras of the Goddess Lalita Tripurasundari selected from the original chant, Lalita Sahasranāma, which appears in the Brahmāṇḍa Purāṇa. The second is a commentary on Dakṣiṇāmūrti Stotram written by Shankara.

Lalita Sahasranāma is revered as a treasure house of the knowledge of Sri Vidya. Seekers of all kinds, yogis, tantrics, and non-dualists alike, are drawn to it. Each name of the Goddess is packed with profound meaning - the gross, the subtle, and the subtlest. Depending on their interest and intent, seekers are drawn spontaneously towards one or the other of the interpretations. In his commentary, Sri Srinivasa Rao draws out the hidden and subtlest of meanings of each name.

Sri Vidya is an ancient and influential Goddess-centered tantric practice that is very much alive in India today. Highly influenced by Shaiva Advaita, Sri Vidya is considered the pinnacle of achievement by practitioners of Shaiva Advaita. By selecting only those names that describe the essential nature of the Goddess, dividing them into two flows, one that describes the Descent (finitude/manifestation) and the other the Ascent (infinitude/unification) of the Goddess, and interpreting them in the light of Shaiva Advaita, Sri Srinivasa Rao makes Advaita the dominant theme of this esoteric text. According to him, "the brahma vidya of Advaita Vedanta is not different from the Sri Vidya of the Shaiva Advaita because both culminate in the union of the finite self with the Infinite."

The second source text of this book, Dakṣiṇāmūrti Stotram, is a crown jewel among Shankara's hymns with the entire Advaita doctrine packed into ten profound verses. Sri Srinivasa Rao titled the original Telugu version of his commentary as *Dakṣiṇāmūrti Pradakṣiṇa*, which translates literally into "Circumambulating Lord Dakṣiṇāmūrti." Although the hymn is titled Dakṣiṇāmūrti, it is not dedicated to the worship of any particular form of the deity

Siva. It succinctly expounds on the nature of the ātmā (self), its relation to the world (jagat), the nature of brahman, and the final bliss of the realization of the ātmān as brahman.

Inspired by the spirit of Advaita that runs through these seemingly different genres of texts (Tantra versus Advaita), I feel inclined to combine them into one book, and present them side-by-side. Sri Srinivasa Rao's penetrating vision did not see any differences in the essential message of these two texts. As Swami Tapasyananda writes in his commentary on Soundarya Lahari ("Waves of Beauty"), an ode to the Goddess, "While the Advaita of Sri Shankara achieves unity by the sublation of the 'many' as a mere appearance, the Shakta Advaita seeks to obtain this by recognizing in the 'many' the manifestation of the One."

I offer this book to all seekers whose hearts are filled with love and devotion for the truth. I hope you will be just as inspired by this translation as I was with the original works of Sri Srinivasa Rao,

– Padma Neppalli
Fremont, CA, USA

The Secret Doctrine in Sri Lalita Divya Nāma

(Sri Lalita Aṣṭottara Rahasyārthamu)

Translation Notes

This commentary is an interpretive translation of the original Telugu commentary written by Sri Yellamraju Srinivasa Rao. The literal one-line translations, additionally provided in this English translation, have been taken from various sources, including sources freely available online and from the printed copy of the *Thousand Names of the Divine Mother* published by Sri Mata Amritanandamayi Trust.

Sometimes a single name of the Goddess has been expounded in each section and other times a collection of related names. The names are sometimes referred to simply as Divine Names and other times as nāma-*s* or mantras. The terms, names, nāma, and mantra have been used interchangeably throughout this book since they all refer to the one Goddess Sri Lalita. The Goddess has also been variously referred to as the Goddess, Devī, Divine Mother, or śakti (energy/ power). Shiva is referred to as śiva, the Supreme Consciousness, whose supreme power is śakti.

The tables in the beginning of chapters 1 and 2 list the order in which the mantras are discussed in this book and their corresponding location in the original 1000 names of the Divine Mother. Note that the locations provided in these tables are approximations only and may vary from publication to publication, since there is no strict order in which the divine names are traditionally chanted.

Author's Preface

I named this book, *Lalita Aṣṭottara Rahasyārthamu* (*The Hidden Meaning in 108 Names of the Goddess Lalita*). Lalita is that which transcends all the worlds. This book describes the divine nature (*devī svarūpa)* of the Goddess Lalita. The root-word *devana* could be interpreted either as divine effulgence or divine play. Consciousness is ever-shining, so Its nature is effulgence. It is commonly referred to as *deva*, God, or the Divine Masculine. When the divine effulgence expands and manifests as the world with myriad names and forms, it is called śakti, Devī, Goddess or the Divine Feminine. Hence, śakti, the creative power of *deva* is Devī. *Śakti śaktimato abheda* – There is no difference between power and the one who wields the power. How can there be any difference between two formless entities? Whatever is *deva* is also *devī*, and whatever is *devī* is also *deva*. Since they are both formless, they are beyond gender. The Upanishads declare that Consciousness is neither feminine nor masculine. Yet, in common parlance, devī or śakti (energy*)* is worshipped as the Divine Feminine, and śiva (Consciousness) as the Divine Masculine (God). Śakti (energy/power) is insentient. It cannot exist independently on its own. It depends on śiva, Consciousness, for its existence. Interestingly, scholars differentiate between śiva and śakti based on the qualities attributed to them. Those who focus on śiva consider śakti (power) as His attribute. Those who focus on śakti consider śiva (Consciousness) as Her attribute. These differences are perceived by the intellect that is used to seeing multiplicity. In essence, there is absolutely no difference between the two. If śiva and śakti were not united as One, śiva would be a śava (corpse) without śakti, and śakti would have no existence without śiva. This Oneness of the apparent two is referred to as śiva-śakti samarasa.

If śakti depends on śiva for its existence, why do ritualists give importance to śakti? The reason is that it is only through śakti that one can attain śiva. It is common experience that it is only through effort (sādya) that one can attain any goal. Without effort, nothing can be attained. This is true not only in worldly matters, but also in matters that transcend the world. There is only one goal for all human beings. And that is to attain śivasāyujya, complete unification with śiva, which means complete dissolution of the separate self in the Universal Self, which is Pure Consciousness. In reality, we are all manifestations of śiva. Therefore, in essence, we are already pure Consciousness, but, due to avidyā (ignorance), we forget this truth. As a result, we identify with the finite objects of the world, feel trapped in the wheel of saṃsāra, and suffer endlessly. If we want to free ourselves from saṃsāra and attain liberation (mokṣa or śiva sāyujya), we must discover the means for doing so. Śakti is the only means or instrument through which we can attain śiva, i.e. realize our true nature.

Why is śakti the only means for liberation? Śakti is the expansion of śiva, the power that flows externally. We can trace the power back to its source. For instance, the rays of the sun expand and reach the earth. The light from the sun rays is visible everywhere. If we enquire into the nature of the light and trace the rays back to its source, we will arrive at the source, which is the sun. The effect (sun rays) points to the cause (sun). This is the operating principle in the world we perceive. The pot is a reminder about the clay which is its source. The cloth is a reminder about the threads which is its source, and the tree is a reminder of the seed from which it germinated. There are many such examples of cause and effect relationships. For every effect we perceive, there is a cause. If we are not able to see the cause, it is only because of our own inability to do so, and not because the cause does not exist.

Śakti is the effect and śiva is the cause. Śiva is Consciousness and śakti is His expansion, energy, or creative power. Hence, using śakti as the means, a seeker can most certainly trace it to its source and attain śiva sāyujya, complete union with śiva. One of the most important names (nāma-s or mantras) of the Goddess is śiva-dūtī, which means "messenger of śiva." Śakti appears like a messenger of śiva. Originally, śakti is completely unified with śiva. In this state, She is called parā. There is no separation whatsoever, no movement or vibration in Her, since She is the Immutable, Infinite Consciousness. When the desire to expand arises in śiva, like a ripple or vibration in the ocean of Pure Consciousness, śakti manifests as His desire - icchā rūpini. In that state, She is known as paśyantī. When the desire transforms into an impetus to act, She is known as madhyama. In the state of madhyama, śakti abandons Her un-manifest state, and manifests instead as the five elements - space, air, water, fire, and earth. In this state, She is known as vaikharī. The phenomenal world we perceive everywhere is the vaikharī form of śakti. She permeates everything, not only the macrocosm (world) that appears outside us, but also the microcosm (thoughts, feelings, and emotions) that appear inside us. In the state of parā, śakti is completely One with śiva. The cause alone IS without an effect. The effect (the three states) appears during Her transformation from the un-manifest to manifest. Of the three states, only the third state vaikharī is visible to us because it is gross. The other two, paśyantī and madhyama, are not visible to us because they are extremely subtle. From the gross and visible, we can infer the subtle and invisible. Therefore, we can grasp parā śakti from Her manifest form (gross world/from her vaikharī). All we need is sincere effort and determination to realize Her.

The nāma, *śivajñāna pradāyini,* means She who offers the knowledge of śiva. If we combine the two nāma-s of the Goddess together, *śiva dūtī* and *śivajñāna pradāyini*, and contemplate on their combined meaning, we will intuitively realize that it is śiva*'s* śakti (power or energy) Itself that has manifested as the world (vaikharī), and that it is the same śakti that can take us back to śiva by bestowing on us the Knowledge of śiva, the Supreme Self, and the complete dissolution of the separate self.

A doubt may arise at this point. How can the Knowledge of the Supreme Self culminate in the complete dissolution of the individual self? Knowledge of the Self is the only means to liberation. This is the truth that all non-dual seekers must understand. Neither the creation of the world nor the entry of the individual into the world ever really happened. It is only due to ignorance, lack of right knowledge, that we think that the individual and the world are real. The analogy of a dream can illustrate this point clearly. Dream is common experience. While dreaming, we forget our waking world and perceive a dream world inside us as though it is external. We wander around in the dream world thinking it is real. But soon as we wake up in the morning and see the waking world, we realize that what we saw in the dream is unreal. We realize that neither the world nor the objects that appeared in the world are real. They never really existed, even though they appeared to exist in the dream. We just have to wake up from the dream. No effort is required to get rid of the dream objects and events, since they never really existed. Similarly, this world appears real only due to ignorance. Ignorance can be destroyed with right Knowledge.

As discussed earlier, although our very nature is Consciousness, we have forgotten this truth. We enter into this dream-like saṃsāra and feel trapped in the vicious cycle of birth and death. We suffer because we forget our real nature. Therefore, just like a dream that disappears on waking up, when the Knowledge of the Self arises, ignorance disappears. Recognizing our true nature as Pure Consciousness is the only practice or sādhana necessary. Forgetfulness and Recollection are the two key words that summarize the problem and the solution. Ignorance and Knowledge are synonymous with forgetfulness and recollection. It is only due to ignorance that we think parāśakti (Supreme Power) has transformed into vaikharī. The philosophers of the sāṅkhya tradition postulate that śakti transformed (pariṇāma) into the world we perceive. Advaita dismisses this idea and instead declares that the world is only an appearance (vivarta). No state can exist independently on its own without a substratum. From the state of parā to the state of vaikharī, throughout the entire 'process' of manifestation, Consciousness is ever present. What does that mean? It means that parā, paśyantī, madhyama, and vaikharī are nothing but Consciousness Itself. Like a rope appearing as a snake or a stick, Consciousness appears as different states. No action is required to get rid of an appearance. Only Knowledge is required. It is due to ignorance that we see vaikharī, and it is through Knowledge that we see parā (Pure Consciousness). Just as light is the solution to darkness, Knowledge is the solution to ignorance. When darkness is removed, everything becomes visible. Similarly, when ignorance is removed, everything will appear in its true nature as Consciousness.

This entire creation is a manifestation of the power of Consciousness (caitanya śakti). It is this Supreme Power that appears as particulars in the micro- and macro-cosmic worlds.

Consciousness is the cause and Its power/śakti is the effect (world) we perceive. Hence, the world we see is nothing but the formless śakti appearing as names and forms. If we continue to contemplate on the world as an appearance of śakti, we will be able to trace It to its source, which is śiva or Pure Consciousness. Initially, when we are entrenched in names and forms, it appears as though śakti is pushing us deep into saṃsāra (tirodhāna). However, as soon as we turn our attention towards the substratum (śiva) on which the names and forms appear, Devī graces (anugraha) us with the Knowledge of śiva. That is why Devī is worshipped as *vidyāvidyāsvarūpini* (She who is of the nature of both Knowledge and ignorance). As avidyā, She conceals our true nature and projects a separate self and a world (not-Self). As vidyā, She removes ignorance and reveals the true nature of the Self and the world. This process - descent into saṃsāra (avidyā) and ascent to śiva (vidyā) - summarizes the nature of śakti.

It is this ascent and descent of śakti that ancient sages like Sage Hayagrīva have revealed to the world through the 1000 names (sahasranāma) of the Goddess Lalita. The significance of these names can be grasped only through intuition and deep insight into their meaning. Hence this chant (sahasranāma) is popularly known as the "secret" (rahasya) chant. Although śakti is śivātmaka, one with śiva, Her real nature is hidden from us. We only see Her manifestation, the saṃsāra around us, and think it is real. We fail to see Her as the substratum that pervades the entire manifestation. The chant reveals Her hidden nature as Pure Consciousness and empowers the seeker with the knowledge of the Self. To reveal this hidden knowledge of the Goddess and clearly explain its significance to the seekers of the world, I have written this commentary on the Divine Names of the Goddess. I have selected only 108 names out of the 1000 names and arranged them in a sequence that can provide an insight into the significance of each name of the Goddess as well as a collection of Her names.

Some scholars may consider my approach a violation to the tradition. However, I assure them that there is no cause for such concern. My approach targets and benefits serious non-dual seekers of the world. For instance, let us consider these two mantras or Divine Names of the Goddess: *nāmapārāyaṇa prīta* and *rahoyāga kramārādhya.* If you delve a little deep into the meaning of these two names, it will soon become clear to you why I took the approach I took. The word pārāyaṇa does not mean, as it is usually understood, as continuous chanting of the nāma-s without a pause. Parā means "shore" (goal), and ayana mean "reaching." So the nāma means "reaching the goal." Every Divine Name of the Goddess has a very specific purpose or goal. The seeker can attain that goal only by chanting the Divine Name meaningfully. Only because each mantra has a specific purpose, this chant is significant. When the Divine Names are chanted with deep insight into their meaning, the Goddess is "pleased" *(prīta)*. Therefore, from this nāma (*nāmapārāyaṇa prīta*), it is clear that the Divine Names of the Goddess are not meant to be chanted mechanically as in a japa, but are meant to be chanted with a deep insight into the truth that they are pointing to.

The nāma or mantra, *rahoyāga kramārādhya,* provides a clue as to how to attain that insight. Rahoyāga means "secret ritual." This ritual is not like the rituals that are performed externally. It is a jñāna yajña, a Knowledge-based ritual or sacrifice. To perform this ritual correctly and win the grace of the Goddess, the appropriate mantras or nāma-s must be chanted in a particular order. Although they are a 1000 names, not every name is unique in its meaning. There are many repetitions, not only in the way they sound but also in their meanings. We find several names that have the same meaning. These names are also chanted in no particular logical order. This becomes very clear once we start paying close attention to the nāma-s and their meaning. This is the reason why I did not try to follow the order in which the names are traditionally chanted. Had I done so, I would merely be complying with the tradition, and not contributing to the right understanding. By not constricting myself to the tradition, I could meet the noble goal set forth by the divine name rahoyāga, which is to draw out the deeper meaning and truth that each name is pointing to, which is the Oneness of śiva and śakti.

Therefore, with seekers of truth (mokṣa) in mind, I selected a few names out of the 1000 names of the Goddess and arranged them in an order that provides a deep insight into the nature of the Goddess, who is our very Self. Coincidentally, I ended up with an auspicious 108 names! Since they are part of the original 1000 names, the 108 names I selected retain their authenticity. I originally wrote this commentary in Sanskrit, but to benefit all Telugu-speaking seekers, I rewrote it in Telugu. However, I don't really feel that I have written this commentary for someone. I feel that I have written it for myself, since, for a long time, I have had a deep longing in my heart to write and extoll, for my own pleasure, the glory of śakti and Her union with śiva.

– Yellamraju Srinivasa Rao,
– Vijayawada, AP, India

Sri Lalita Divya Nama

Following tables present the selected 108 mantras discussed in this book and their corresponding approximate location in the original Lalita Sahasranāma.

अवरोहण (Descent)

#	दिव्य नाम	No.	#	दिव्य नाम	No.
1	श्री माता	*1*	28	तिरोधानकरीश्वरी	*270*
2	श्री महाराज्ञी	*2*	29	सदाशिवानुग्रहदा	*272*
3	श्रीमत्-सिंहासनेश्वरी	*3*	30	विश्वरूपा, जागरिणी,	*256*
4	चिदग्नि कुण्डसम्भूता	*4*	31	स्वपन्ती, तैजसात्मिका	*258*
5	चिदेक रसरूपिणी	*364*	32	सुप्ता, प्राज्ञात्मिका	*260*
6	अप्रमेया	*413*	33	तुर्या, सर्वावस्था विवर्जिता	*262*
7	स्वप्रकाशा	*414*	34	भवचक्र प्रवर्तिनी	*843*
8	सर्वगा	*702*	35	सुधासागर मध्यस्था	*61*
9	सर्वोपाधि विनिर्मुक्ता	*708*	36	कदम्ब वनवासिनी	*60*
10	महामाया	*215*	37	कुलरूपिणी	*897*
11	महाशक्ति	*217*	38	त्वक्स्था	*481*
12	इच्छाशक्ति ज्ञानशक्ति क्रियाशक्ति स्वरूपिणी	*658*	39	रुधिर संस्थिता	*490*
13	चिच्छक्ति, श्चेतनारूपा	*416*	40	मांसनिष्ठा	*500*
14	जडशक्ति, र्जडात्मिका	*418*	41	मेदोनिष्ठा	*509*
15	अनेककोटि ब्रह्माण्ड जननी	*620*	42	अस्थिसंस्थिता	*516*
16	आब्रह्म कीटजननी	*285*	43	मज्जासंस्था	*524*

#	दिव्य नाम	No.	#	दिव्य नाम	No.
17	परा, प्रत्यक्चिती रूपा	*366*	44	शुक्ल संस्थिता	*531*
18	पश्यन्ती, परदेवता	*368*	45	सुमेरु मध्यशृङ्गस्था	*55*
19	मध्यमा	*370*	46	चिन्तामणि गृहान्तस्था	*57*
20	वैखरीरूपा	*371*	47	ज्ञानविग्रहा	*644*
21	तत्त्वाधिका, तत्त्वमयी	*906*	48	आत्मा	*617*
22	चराचर जगन्नाथा	*244*	49	आबालगोप विदिता	*994*
23	सर्वानुल्लङ्घ्य शासना	*995*	50	मनोरूपेक्षुकोदण्डा	*10*
24	पञ्चकृत्य परायणा	*274*	51	पञ्चतन्मात्र सायका	*11*
25	सृष्टिकर्त्री, ब्रह्मरूपा	*264*	52	रागस्वरूप पाशाढ्या	*8*
26	गोप्त्री, गोविन्दरूपिणी	*266*	53	क्रोधाकाराङ्शोज्ज्वला	*9*
27	संहारिणी, रुद्ररूपा	*268*	54	सर्वमोहिनी	*703*

आरोहण (Ascent)

#	दिव्य नाम	No.	#	दिव्य नाम	No.
1	अव्याज करुणामूर्ति	992	28	निर्भेदा	178
2	देवकार्यसमुद्यता	5	29	भेदनाशिनी	179
3	शिवदूती,	408	30	निर्ममा,	164
4	गुरुमूर्ति	603	31	निरहङ्कारा	161
5	शास्त्रसारा	845	32	मृत्युमथनी	181
6	शिवज्ञान प्रदायिनी	727	33	निर्भवा	174
7	पशुपाश विमोचनी	354	34	शान्ता	141
8	मुक्तिदा	736	35	ब्राह्मी	675
9	बहिर्मुख सुदुर्लभा	871	36	परानिष्ठा	573
10	अन्तर्मुख समाराध्या	870	37	हेयोपादेय वर्जिता	304
11	मिथ्या जगदधिष्ठाना	735	38	अभ्यासाति शयज्ञाता	990
12	विद्याऽविद्या स्वरूपिणी	402	39	मैत्र्यादि वासनालभ्या	570

#	दिव्य नाम	No.	#	दिव्य नाम	No.
13	दुष्टदूरा	193	40	अज्ञानध्वान्त दीपिका	993
14	शिष्टेष्टा	411	41	ज्ञानज्ञेय स्वरूपिणी	981
15	संहृताशेष पाषण्डा	355	42	सामरस्य परायणा	792
16	सदाचार प्रवर्तिका	356	43	स्वस्था	914
17	समयाचार तत्परा	98	44	एकाकिनी	665
18	सम्प्रदायेश्वरी	710	45	दुःखहन्त्री	191
19	महाविद्या	584	46	पुरुषार्थप्रदा	291
20	ब्रह्मात्मैक्य स्वरूपिणी	672	47	स्वर्गापवर्गदा	764
21	तत्त्वमर्थ स्वरूपिणी	908	48	निर्वाण सुखदायिनी	390
22	विमर्शरूपिणी	548	49	सद्यः प्रसादिनी	383
23	परापरा	790	50	यजमान स्वरूपिणी	883
24	प्रसिद्धा	395	51	सर्वान्तर्यामिनी	819
25	भावनागम्या	113	52	पूर्णा	292
26	ध्यानगम्या	641	53	शाश्वती	951
27	ध्यानध्यातृ ध्येयरूपा	254	54	श्री शिवा	998

CHAPTER 1

The Descent

In this chapter, the descent of the Goddess from the state of Pure Un-manifest Consciousness to the manifest world are described in 54 nāma-s. The table below lists the nāma-s and their approximate location in the original sahasranāma (1000 names of the Goddess).

#	**Divine Name** (nāma)	**No.**	#	**Divine Name** (nāma)	**No.**
1	śri mātā	*1*	28	tirōdhānakarīśvarī	*270*
2	śri mahārājñī	*2*	29	sadāśivānugrahadā	*272*
3	śrīmat-siṃhāsanēśvarī	*3*	30	viśvarūpā, jāgariṇī,	*256*
4	chidagni kuṇḍasambhūtā	*4*	31	svapantī, taijasātmikā	*258*
5	chidēka rasarūpiṇī	*364*	32	suptā, prājñātmikā,	*260*
6	apramēyā	*413*	33	turyā, sarvāvasthā vivarjitā	*262*
7	svaprakāśā	*414*	34	bhavachakra pravartini	*843*
8	sarvagā	*702*	35	sudhāsāgara madhyasthā	*61*
9	sarvōpādhi vinirmuktā	*708*	36	kadamba vanavāsinī	*60*
10	mahāmāyā	*215*	37	kularūpiṇī	*897*
11	mahāśakti	*217*	38	tvaksthā	*481*
12	icchāśakti jñānaśakti kriyāśakti svarūpiṇī	*658*	39	rudhira saṃsthitā	*490*
13	citśakti, chētanārūpā	*416*	40	māṃsaniṣṭhā	*500*
14	jaḍaśakti, jaḍātmikā	*418*	41	mēdōniṣṭhā	*509*
15	anēkakōṭi brahmāṇḍa jananī	*620*	42	asthisaṃsthitā	*516*
16	ābrahma kīṭajananī	*285*	43	majjāsaṃsthā	*524*

#	**Divine Name** (nāma)	**No.**	#	**Divine Name** (nāma)	**No.**
17	parā, pratyakchitī rūpā	*366*	44	śukla saṃsthitā	*531*
18	paśyantī, paradēvatā	*368*	45	sumēru madhyaśṛṅgasthā	*55*
19	madhyamā	*370*	46	chintāmaṇi gṛhāntasthā	*57*
20	vaikharīrūpā	*371*	47	jñānavigrahā	*644*
21	tattvādhikā, tattvamayī	*906*	48	ātmā	*617*
22	carācara jagannāthā	*244*	49	ābālagōpa viditā	*994*
23	sarvānullaṅghya śāsanā	*995*	50	manōrūpēkṣukōdaṇḍā	*10*
24	pañchakṛtya parāyaṇā	*274*	51	pañchatanmātra sāyakā	*11*
25	sṛṣṭikartrī, brahmarūpā	*264*	52	rāgasvarūpa pāśāḍhyā	*8*
26	gōptrī, gōvindarūpiṇī	*266*	53	krōdhākārāṅkuśōjjvalā	*9*
27	saṃhāriṇī, rudrarūpā	*268*	54	sarvamōhinī	*703*

1. śrī mātā 2. śri mahārājñī 3. śrīmat-siṃhāsanēśvarī

She who is the Auspicious mother.
She who is the Empress of the Universe.
She who is Ruler of the most glorious throne.

We find these nāma-s or mantras in the original Lalita sahasranāma (1000 names of the Goddess) as well as in Lalita aṣṭottara nāma (108 names of the Goddess). They symbolize the creation (mātā), sustenance (mahārājñī), and dissolution (siṃhāsanēśvarī) of the world. While the first two names may not raise any questions, the last one is most likely to. The name siṃhāsanēśvarī literally translates into "She who rules the world sitting on a glorious lion-shaped throne." The literal translation does not explicitly say anything about "dissolution," so we must go beyond the literal meaning of the nāma to discover its deeper significance. Siṃhā means lion, that which destroys. Āsan means "to steal." Like a ferocious lion that can destroy anything, the Goddess is capable of destroying the entire world. Hence, siṃhāsanēśvarī implies dissolution.

By describing the Goddess as performing the three functions of creation, sustenance, and dissolution, sages have established that Devi is the material cause of this entire universe. Just like the clay that pervades the entire pot, śakti pervades the entire universe. Therefore, śakti is the material cause of the universe. Like the pot that is not different from the clay, the universe is not different from śakti. However, śakti (power or energy) cannot exist independently on its own. Śakti depends on śiva for Her existence. Energy depends on Consciousness for its existence. She is citrūpini, the power of Consciousness. Hence, She is not only the material cause of the universe, She is also the efficient cause because She is "Conscious Power." Therefore, this entire creation is an expression of the union of śakti and śiva, and must be perceived from that viewpoint only. Note that the three mantras share the common prefix śri, although the rest of the words in the mantras are different. The word śri means āśraya or "depend." Śakti (power) depends on Consciousness. It cannot exist on its own. That is why the prefix "śri" is permanently assigned to Devī . The differences (in the rest of the words) in the mantras symbolize the transitory nature of the world. The world is only an appearance, an illusion that appears on an Immutable substratum called Consciousness. Hence, Consciousness alone is Real. Everything else is only an appearance, therefore, unreal.

Since the world has no real existence of its own, we cannot look upon it as saṃsāra or bondage either. Instead, we must look upon it as an appearance of śakti, the intrinsic power of Consciousness. The more we contemplate on śakti in this manner, the closer She will take us to śiva, which is our real nature. Śakti is brahmavidyā, the Supreme Knowledge of brahman or Pure Consciousness. Only through vidyā (Knowledge) can one realize śiva (Self). The goal of human life is to realize the true nature of the Self. Śakti can help us attain that goal. Hence, unlike the tantrics (ritualists), Advaitins believe that Sri Vidyā (knowledge of the Goddess) is brahmavidyā itself. There is no difference between the two.

Another interesting detail to note is the *m* syllable next to the syllable śri. When the two syllables (śri + *m*) are pronounced together in the three mantras as "śrim," we repeatedly hear the "*m*" sound. This is not a coincidence. It is by design and intention of Sage Hayagriva who compiled the 1000 names of the Goddess. Śrim is a mantra of the Goddess Soḍaśī, who personifies brahmavidyā, the Knowledge of the Supreme Self. The syllable *m* points directly to the eternal brahman. Repeated and meaningful chanting of śrim śrim śrim produces brahmākāra vṛtti, a thought modification in the form of brahman. The thought of brahman purifies the mind. The goal is to attain brahmavidyā through a purified mind, word, and deed. Only then the mantra produces a three-fold result. That is why Sage Hayagriva chanted this mantra (śri) not only in the beginning but also at the end of the Sri Lalitha chant – *śrī chakrarājanilayā, śrīmat tripura sundarī, śri śivā.* Through repetition, the Sage is emphasizing the significance of śrividyā, making it clear that there is no difference between śrividyā and brahmavidyā, and that śrividyā leads one to śivasāyujya, the ultimate union of the individual self with the Supreme Self.

4. chidagni kuṇḍasambhūtā

She who is born in the fire-pit of Pure Consciousness.

How can we say śakti, which is brahmavidyā itself, is the only means for attaining śiva sāyujya? This fourth mantra answers this question. Śakti rises from the fire pit of Pure Consciousness (śiva). She is in complete union with śiva at all times. That is why She is called śivam. She is Existence (*sat*). He is Consciousness (*cīt*). It is impossible, even for a moment, śakti (Existence) to forsake śiva (Consciousness). If śakti distances Herself from śiva, She will become inert. When an object loses contact with Consciousness, the object will cease to exist. For an object to exist, it must be known to Consciousness. Everything, from the earth to the vast space, exists only because it is cognized by Consciousness. If a thing does not appear to our Consciousness, it ceases to exist. Consciousness is the witness to the existence of everything. Therefore, śakti can be known only through śiva (Consciousness). We must live in this phenomenal world deeply aware of our real nature as Consciousness. The word sambhūtā in the mantra indicates this. Sometimes this word is interpreted in its secondary meaning as "being born." The primary meaning of the word, however, is "union," the union of śakti and śiva. The primary meaning is most appropriate in this context.

5. chidēka rasarūpiṇī

She who is of the nature of pure Knowledge.

Some think caitanya śakti implies two separate entities, power and Consciousness. We should not make such a mistake in the context of parāvidyā, the Supreme Knowledge that transcends all duality because It is the One and only substance that IS. It is both caitanya and śakti, Consciousness and Existence, Intelligence and Energy. This mantra conveys this meaning beautifully. The word *rasa* in this mantra means nature. The word eka means identical nature. Consciousness is the very nature of everything. Therefore, Consciousness is not different from its Power. Even if we hear the two words spoken separately, we must remember that the two are referring to the one substance. It is like saying "a flame of fire." Both flame and fire refer to the same thing. Similarly, caitanya and śakti refer to the same thing. The flame belongs to the fire. Similarly, power belongs to Consciousness. Power and the One who wields the power are not two separate entities. Hence, in every reference to śakti is an implied reference to śiva. Instead of perceiving forms as śakti, the seeker must contemplate on śakti as the formless Consciousness.

6. apramēyā

She who cannot be measured by the sense organs.

Since śakti is formless Consciousness, She is *apramēyā*. She cannot be grasped by any instrument of knowledge, such as the five senses. For an object to exist, it must be cognized by a cognizing instrument. If it cannot be cognized, the object has no existence. When we say something exists, it is only because we are aware of its existence through the medium of our sense organs. When we say the pot exists, the cloth exists, etc., we say so because we are aware of their existence. How do we become aware? We see with our eyes, we hear with our ears, we touch with our skin, and taste with our tongue. Hence, it is the sense organs that are the instruments with which we perceive objects. This is called pratyakṣa pramāṇa, direct perception of objects. One the other hand, when we see smoke rising on a distant hill, we know that there is fire on the hill, even though we do not see the fire directly. Based on what is visible to our eyes, we infer the existence of what is not visible. We see smoke, and from the smoke, we deduce the existence of fire. This indirect or inferential knowledge is called anumāna pramāṇa.

Therefore, direct and indirect perception are the only two natural means of knowledge that humans have. We are born with five external facing sense organs and one internal organ called the mind. The former are direct means of knowledge and the latter is an indirect means of knowledge. With our eyes, we perceive smoke on the mountain, and with our mind, we infer the existence of fire. We acquire the knowledge of every object in the world only through these two means.

However, these means fail in the context of Consciousness. Consciousness cannot be known either through direct or indirect perception because It is not an object. Therefore, it cannot be perceived by the senses or the mind. Hence it is aprameÿā. If it cannot be known through any of these means, how can we prove its existence? Even if the mind and sense organs cannot perceive Consciousness, Its existence cannot be denied because Consciousness is Awareness Itself. Every means of perception, direct or indirect, in reality is Consciousness only. It is only to Consciousness or Awareness that everything is known. Consciousness flows out through our sense organs to the external world of objects, through our mind to our internal feelings of pleasure and pain, and knows everything. Without Consciousness, our eyes would not see and ears would not hear. If our sense organs are working, it means Consciousness is operating through them. Hence, Consciousness is the ultimate means of knowledge. No instrument is necessary to know Consciousness. It is just like a lamp that does not require another lamp to illumine it. Consciousness is the knower of everything. If we insist on finding a means to prove the existence of Consciousness, we will be attributing both doer-ship and action to the one and same entity. An entity cannot be both a doer of an action as well as the action itself. Fire cannot burn itself! Similarly, Consciousness is aware of the external world and internal feelings, but It cannot be aware of Itself, since it is Awareness itself! Hence, Devī, is referred to as aprамēyā, the one who cannot be cognized through sense organs.

7. svaprakāśā

She who is self-luminous.

An object exists only if it is known to a cognizing intelligence. This is true in the phenomenal realm, but not true in the realm of śakti, since śakti is not an object. Śakti is Consciousness, the subject that knows all objects. When the subject is Consciousness itself, there is no need for another entity to vouch for its existence. Consciousness is Self-evident. While the whole world is known to Consciousness, Consciousness knows Itself through the ever-present "I Am" awareness. Because It is aware of Its own Beingness, śakti is svaprakāśā, self-luminous. No doer-ship or activity can be attributed to It. Unlike fire which is inert and unaware of its own nature (its ability to burn other things), śakti is the Supreme Power of the Supreme Consciousness, so It is Self-Evident and Self-Luminous.

Hence, śakti is both the subject and the object. She is apramēyā because She is the subject and cannot be known through any means of knowledge. Since She is *svaprakāśā*, She knows Herself through Herself.

8. sarvagā

She who pervades all the worlds and all living and non-living things. She who is omnipresent.

Only Consciousness can shine both as the subject and the object. Because It is aware of Itself, It is both pramāṇa (means of knowledge) and pramēyā (object of knowledge). Inert objects, such as space are not self-aware. They depend on a source of knowledge or a knower for their existence. It is only Consciousness that reveals the five elements to us. If it were not for Consciousness, this entire universe would appear as nothing but darkness. If inert objects cannot cognize their own existence and there is no Conscious entity to cognize their existence, what else could be there except darkness? Therefore the entire world of objects depends on Consciousness for its existence, but Consciousness exists on its own. It shines and makes everything shine in its effulgence. Hence, the Goddess is called *sarvagā* - that which is expansive and permeates everything, living and non-living. Expansion does not mean external expansion only. It means inside, outside, and in the middle. Everything appears in Consciousness. There can be nothing outside Consciousness. If an object loses touch with Consciousness, it ceases to exist. For a thing to be known in its entirety, it must be pervaded in its entirety by Consciousness. Śakti is the source of this entire universe. Because

She is Consciousness Itself, the universe appears to us. Because of Her infinite and expansive nature, we revere Her as *sarvagā*.

9. sarvōpādhi vinirmuktā

She who is free from all limitations.

When we say śakti pervades everything (names and forms), we should not assume that they are really existing separately, and śakti pervades them. This mantra removes this misconception. Names and forms are upādhi-s, adjuncts through which śakti expresses itself. But śakti is not limited or restrained in any way by these upādhi-s. Consciousness is the subject and these are objects known to It. Although we refer to them as this and that (subject and object), in reality, there are no two separate entities. There is only Consciousness, and It is cognizing Itself! When Consciousness is cognizing something, It becomes the "subject." When It is cognizing Itself, it becomes an object. Hence, Consciousness is both the subject that knows as well as the object that is known. Only Consciousness is capable of playing the two roles as the subject and the object. Hence, it is a mistake to consider the world as separate from Consciousness. Whatever we perceive as "existing" is Consciousness only. The divine name of the Goddess, *vijñāna ghana rūpini*, reveals this truth. When we think of gold, the image of a solid mass of gold comes to our mind. Similarly, *vijñāna ghana rūpini* means Devī is nothing but Pure Knowledge or Pure Consciousness. The word "nothing" refers to the illusory and transitory names and forms that appear to us. These are only the upādhi-s, the instruments through which Consciousness appears as objects to us, but neither the objects nor the upādhi-s have any real existence of their own.

A thing that is superimposed on another thing is an upādhi. According to Advaita, a superimposition can occur in two ways.

A book placed on top of a table is one type of superimposition. A wooden log that appears as a plank is another type of superimposition. In the former case, the book and the table are two separate objects, one superimposed on the other. In the latter case, the wooden log and the plank are not two separate objects. The log is the plank and the plank is the log. Aside from the log, there is no separate plank to be seen. If a plank is seen in the place of a log, it is not because a plank really exists. It is only because of an optical illusion. All that really is, is a log of wood, but the log can appear either as a log of wood or a plank. This is true of Consciousness as well.

Consciousness is the only substance that IS. Names and forms (upādhi-s) are only Its appearance. They do not have an independent existence of their own. Names and forms are like the plank that is superimposed on the log, and not like the book that is superimposed on a table. The book is different from the table. The plank is not different from the log. It only appears as though it is. The log itself appears both as a log and the plank. Similarly, the upādhi-s, names and forms, we see everywhere, do not really exist as separate entities. They are superimposed on Consciousness. Just like the plank that is not different from the log, names and forms are not different from Consciousness. Pure Consciousness Itself appears as the names and forms. As the seer, Consciousness is the subject. As an appearance (world), it is an object.

In reality, the names and forms we perceive do not exist, not even as a superimposition. Since we are used to seeing duality, we think the world is an upādhi superimposed on Consciousness. In reality, however, the world neither exists nor is it superimposed on Consciousness. When a thing is known only to Consciousness and ceases to exist if it loses touch with Consciousness, how can it be real? It cannot be real! Yet we perceive objects as though they are real!

Why do we perceive objects when they are unreal? The truth is that we do not really see objects. We only see Consciousness appearing as objects (names and forms), just like the ocean appearing as waves and froth. Since śakti or Consciousness itself appears as the upādhi-s (names and forms), She is *sarvōpādhi vinirmuktā - She who is free of all limitations.* That means there are no upādhi-s whatsoever separate from Consciousness. All that IS, is Pure Consciousness.

10. mahāmāyā

She who is the Great Illusion

If these *upādhi*-s are non-existing, why do we continue to see them? If a thing is non-existing, like the horn of a rabbit or the son of a barren women, it should not be appearing to us. The nāma *mahāmāyā* answers this question. Devī is the great illusion. She is the mahāmāyā. She is both the power and the wielder of the power. As śakti, She is the great illusory power called māyā. As śiva, She is the Consciousness that wields the power. Māyā measures the Infinite and makes it appear as though finite. Time, space, and objects are the manifestations of māyā.

If Consciousness alone is Real and everything else is false, what are time and space? How do they measure or limit the Infinite? Are they like the water in a mirage, mere appearances? According to Shiva Advaita, śiva molded Himself into time, space, and the world we perceive. He is like the magician who performs his magic all by himself. Sometimes the magician appears to sit with us, sometimes he appears to run away from us, sometimes he appears to crawl up a rope, sometimes he appears to fall flat and die, and sometimes he suddenly he gets up and smiles at us. He appears to be performing to a script, playing multiple roles and manifesting multiple objects simultaneously. Mesmerized by his performance, we watch in wonder without blinking our eyes.

The example of a magician may be hard for us to relate to if we have never witnessed such a performance. The example of a dream may better illustrate the point. Dream experience is common to all of us. In a dream, we find ourselves in different situations and transacting with different objects. Where did all these dream objects and situations appear from? They all appeared from our Consciousness. Consciousness, as it were, differentiated Itself and appeared in all these forms. On waking up, when we realize it was all a dream, we are amazed at how real the dream objects appeared in the dream. This is the māyā we experience in our daily lives – perceiving an illusion and thinking it is real.

When we cannot fathom the māyā that we experience in our individual lives, how can we fathom mahāmāyā, the great illusion, that is operating at the cosmic level? Mahāmāyā transcends worldly māyā-s. A magician in the world, with his limited power, can perform a few magic tricks with a sleight of hand or through hypnosis. He may also use some tools to perform his tricks, even though the tools may not be visible to us. However, Devī , the Supreme Power, does not need any tools. Since She is formless, there is no scope for any 'sleight of hand.' Since the performance and the spectators watching the performance are not different from Her, there is no need for hypnotism. Without any tools and without any deception, śakti molds Herself into all these forms, sees Herself in all the forms, and transacts with Herself. The great illusion is that we perceive transient names and forms as though they are real, and overlook the only real substance that IS. We don't doubt our experience. It is like saying we see a black sky or that the sky is black. From the perspective of the individual, who sees the unreal as though it is real (ex: seeing black in the formless empty space we call sky) is ignorance. From the perspective of māyā śakti, the unreal appearing as though it is real is a projection or an appearance.

11. mahāśakti

She who has great power.

Māyā presents the impossible as possible and the possible as impossible. While remaining in its intrinsic nature as the formless śakti, it can manifest in any form. This is the essential nature of śakti. It is through Her expansion and Her manifestation that we know or recognize Her. As Svetaśvatara Upanishad states: "The Vedas speak of His exalted power, which is innate and capable of producing diverse effects, and also of His omniscience and might."

Śakti manifests as the phenomenal world and moves freely without any restraint. She is the invisible current in the ocean that manifests externally as waves, bubbles, foam, etc. She is the hidden energy in the tree that manifests externally as branches, leaves, flowers, and fruits. Hence, śakti is present inside every object as energy and outside as name and form.

Mahāśakti transcends the phenomenal world. It is the Supreme Power of Consciousness that manifests as the micro- and macro-cosmic worlds containing countless sentient and insentient entities. We stare in awe at the ever-changing spectacular universe. When it is un-manifest or dormant, like the invisible current in the ocean, we call it śakti. When it manifests externally as names and forms, like the waves in the ocean, we call it māyā. Śakti and māyā are both a play of Consciousness.

12. icchāśakti, jñānaśakti, kriyāśakti svarūpiṇī

She who is in the form of the powers of will, knowledge, and action.

How does that one primordial energy manifest in so many forms? How does it perpetuate so many changes? This mantra answers this question.

Although śakti is a single entity, It has many aspects. The very nature of śakti is change. It changes or transforms in three ways. Originally śakti is in the form of jñāna or Consciousness. The mantra, *chidēka rasarūpiṇī,* indicates this. Since śakti is Consciousness, It is independent. Because It is independent, It can freely manifest or change forms at Its will (icchā). Will or intention is an attribute of Knowledge or Awareness. Therefore, unlike the inert forms of energy we perceive in the phenomenal world, such as electricity, śakti is Conscious Power. Atomic energy and electricity cannot function freely on their own. They depend on a Conscious entity to function. Śakti, the Supreme Power of Consciousness, on the other hand, has the freedom to function on Its own as well as to enable other entities to function. It is distinct from everything, and everything ceases to exist if śakti is absent.

Knowledge (jñāna śakti) transforms into desire or intention, and desire (icchā śakti) transforms into action or the power to act (kriyā śakti). As pure Consciousness, śakti remains undifferentiated and absorbed in Itself. When the desire to expand arises, the desire transforms into action. Every action produces a result. This saṃsāra, the world we perceive, is the result of such action. Action and the result are for the enjoyment of the jīvā, the individual. The jīvā is therefore the bhokta, the enjoyer of the world and its pleasures and pains.

Therefore, the world is the result of the transformation of śakti, from the Infinite and un-manifest to the finite and manifest. Desire, action, result, and experience are the four milestones in this journey. Jñāna śakti or Consciousness is the inner current or underlying substratum through every stage of transformation. Like an expert dancer, parā śakti, the Supreme Consciousness, plays multiple roles. An earnest seeker must contemplate relentlessly on the parāśakti that permeates every object and transaction. As our contemplation continues without a break, identification with the body and mind reduces. Although, in reality, Consciousness (jñāna śakti) precedes desire (icchā śakti) and action (kriyā śakti), this mantra starts with the word icchā to highlight the importance of the icchā śakti of the Goddess over the jñāna śakti of the Lord. Because icchā śakti, the desire to expand, is the source of creation, the mantra starts with the word icchā. Therefore it is by design, and not in error, that this mantra has been formulated in this manner.

13. citśakti-cētanārūpā

She who is the power of Consciousness; She who is Pure Consciousness

As stated earlier, jñāna śakti (Consciousness) transforms first into icchā (will) and then into kriyā (action and results) This mantra explains the manner in which śakti manifests as action and the result of the action. Cītśakti is another name for jñāna śakti. Because it is Consciousness Itself, citśakti manifests as the conscious beings of the world. Consciousness combined with the vital force (prāṇa) that makes humans, animals, and other living beings sentient.

Hence citśakti is the cause and the source of this visible universe. Since She manifested as the world on Her own will and pervades it, from the absolute standpoint, citśakti is both the efficient and the material cause of the world. In the relative world, we find that the efficient cause is different from the material cause. For instance, clay is the material cause of the pot, which is different from the potter who is the efficient cause of the pot. Gold is the material cause of the ornaments, which is different from the goldsmith who is the efficient cause of the ornaments. However, there are no such differences between the material and efficient causes in the Absolute Reality. Since Consciousness or śakti is the Absolute Reality, It is both the efficient and the material cause of the world.

Therefore, all sentient beings that appear as separate entities are, in reality, the universal citśakti only appearing in various forms. They are like the pots that appear as separate objects, although in reality they are all nothing but clay. The two mantras, *citśakti* and *cētanārūpā,* reveal this truth – that śakti or Consciousness is the source of both the sentient and insentient entities of the world. The mantra *citśakti* indicates the efficient cause and the mantra *cētanārūpā* indicates the material cause. That means Consciousness permeates the entire creation as śakti and manifests as the sentient beings of the world. Therefore, a seeker must contemplate on the entire sentient world as citśakti.

14. jaḍaśakti-jaḍātmikā

She who is māyā that has transformed itself as the power of creation; She who is in the form of the inanimate world.

Devī is both citśakti, sentient power, and jadaśakti, insentient power. She is sentient because She is *chidēka rasarūpiṇī,* the one whose nature is pure Knowledge or Awareness. How can She who is of the nature of sentiency also be of the opposite nature, insentient? Although śakti is Conscious Power, She appears as though inert and insentient in the macrocosm as the five elements, and in the microcosm as body, vital force, etc.

Śakti, without undergoing any transformation, manifests in its intrinsic form as Consciousness in humans and other sentient beings. The difference between the various beings is only in the quantity of sentiency they each manifest, and not in the quality of sentiency present in them. While appearing as space and other elements, śakti appears to have transformed itself so much so that its intrinsic nature as Consciousness becomes hidden, and the objects it manifests as become visible and inert. Just because objects appear inert, it does not mean that they are devoid of Consciousness. It is just that, during the manifestation, śakti moves so far away from its original nature as pure Consciousness that it appears as though it is inert. However, an object is never totally inert. If it is totally inert and has lost complete touch with Consciousness, the object would not appear at all. Inert objects, such as buildings, mountains, pots, etc., continue to appear to us because they retain a touch of Consciousness, even though Consciousness manifests only minimally in them.

That is why the energy that permeates these insentient objects is called jaḍa śakti or inert energy. This inert energy is also infused by Consciousness. In the Devī Bhāgavata Purāṇa, the Goddess herself declared to the demon Mahishasura as follows: "Although I am originally inert as śakti, because of my close association with śiva at all times, I am Conscious. I am cit-rūpini, not jaḍa-rūpini."

The Goddess pervades the entire phenomenal world with Her jaḍa śakti (inert power). Hence, when we see an inert object, we must remember that it is śakti Itself appearing as the inert object. Because of Her will (icchā śakti) to expand and manifest as the sentient and insentient objects of the world, Devī is the efficient cause. Because of Her ability to expand and manifest in myriad forms (kriya śakti),

She is the material cause of the world. Therefore, this entire world we perceive is only an expression of Her divine will.

15. anēkakōṭi brahmāṇḍa jananī

She who is the creator of the multitude of worlds.

Consciousness pervades every object internally and externally. Therefore, the essential nature of this entire universe of sentient and insentient objects is śakti. This mantra explains how śakti manifests as the sentient and insentient world.

Brahmāṇḍa means space. There are innumerable objects, such as the sun, moon, stars, and planets, contained in space. Humans inhabit one such space called the earth and are completely absorbed in it. There are countless such spaces and universes. Human mind will draw a blank if it tries to imagine the number of objects contained in each universe. One can only marvel at the power of Consciousness that effortlessly manifests these universes. It is beyond human capacity to describe the magnificence of śakti. Only śakti can describe Her splendor.

16. ābrahma kīṭajananī

She is the mother of everything, from brahma to the lowest of insects.

The Divine Mother is not only the mother of the insentient world. She is also the mother of the sentient world, from a lowly insect such as an ant or a mosquito, to the great creator Brahma, the ruler of satya loka. While the earlier nāma describes the vastness of the insentient world Devī created, this nāma describes the vastness of the sentient world She created. Consciousness does not undergo any change while manifesting sentient beings. The difference is only in the extent to which it (Consciousness) manifests in each sentient form.

According to Hindu mythology, there are a total of fourteen loka-s (worlds) in the universe, seven in the upper sphere and seven in the lower sphere of the universe. There are countless types of living beings of human, divine, and demonic natures living in these worlds. There are also countless types of animals, birds, reptiles, etc. living in these words. It is said that it is impossible even for the creator Brahma to keep track of the actions, perceptions, and feelings of these countless beings. One can only imagine the enormous power of mahāśakti who manifests and sustains these sentient and insentient worlds. Before appearing externally, these worlds were hidden in Her (mahāśakti) womb. The nāma-s *viśvagarbhā* (She who contains the whole world in Her womb) and *svarṇagarbhā* (She who is the cause of the universe) signify this. The word viśva refers to the inert world. The word svarṇa refers to the Conscious world, which is also known as hiraṇyagarbha. Before manifestation, the two worlds are present in the womb of the mahāśakti as pure un-manifested Consciousness. When the desire to expand arose like a ripple in the ocean of Consciousness, śakti moved from Her un-manifest state to the manifest state. The sentient and insentient worlds we perceive are, therefore, only an appearance of that mahāśakti. As manifest or un-manifest, they are all contained in Her womb and cannot transcend It.

17. parā, pratyakchitī rūpā; 18. paśyantī, paradēvatā

She who is Supreme; She who transcends all - She who is of the nature of un-manifested Consciousness.
She who sees - She who is the supreme deity.

How did the un-manifest become manifest? These mantras describe the process. The un-manifest becomes manifest in four stages. The first stage is parā, un-manifested Supreme Power, the inner-most core (pratayak) of manifestation. This mantra corresponds to the mantra *chidēka rasarūpiṇī*. Consciousness (*cit*) is always pratyak (innermost reality), not parāk (external appearance). If Consciousness were also of the nature of parāk, Consciousness would become an object. Because it is formless awareness, Consciousness is ever the subject and never the object. This pure Consciousness is called parā.

As long as the parā śakti (Supreme power) is in complete union with śiva (Supreme Consciousness), there is no vibration (spandana) or movement in its intrinsic power. When the desire to manifest or expand arises in parā śakti, a corresponding vibration appears in its intrinsic nature. This vibration or desire (icchā) to expand is called paśyantī. Hence, icchā śakti is the second stage in the transformation of the parā śakti into the manifested world. While parā is Pure Consciousness, paśyantī is the movement towards expansion. We see this principle operating in the empirical world as well. Before desire in the form of a thought arises in our mind, the mind is still. As soon as the thought arises, we sense a disturbance in the previously still mind. Similarly, the moment the impulse to create arises, the Goddess (śakti) moves from the state of parā to paśyantī.

19. madhyamā; 20. vaikharīrūpā

She who stays in the middle.
She who is of the nature of vaikharī (sound in the form of the manifest world).

The third stage that follows paśyantī is madhyamā. For desire to transform into action, śakti takes the form of kriyā śakti. Since She is in the middle, in transition from icchā to kriyā, at this stage, śakti is called madhyamā. The gross world is not manifest at this stage. It is only a subtle and 'un-blossomed' potential in madhyamā.

When śakti moves from *madhyamā* to *vaikharī*, She blossoms fully. The universe appears with all its tantalizing and transitory forms. This gross appearance of śakti is vaikharī. In Her subtlest form, as un-manifest śakti, She is parā; In Her grossest form as the manifest world, She is vaikharī; and in the in-between states, She is *madhyamā*. In this manner, śakti transitions from the un-manifest and un-differentiated state of Pure Consciousness to the fully manifest and differentiated gross world we perceive.

21. tattvādhikā - tattvamayī

She who transcends all cosmic categories.
She who is reality itself; She who is Siva Himself.

Although we refer to śakti as manifest and un-manifest, in reality, there is no such difference. Śakti is one, not two. At every stage in Her journey from parā to vaikharī, She shines as Pure Consciousness. The apparent stages do not impinge on Her real nature in any way. She does not undergo any change. Her essential nature is Existence-Consciousness, *sat-cit*. Since *sat* and *cit* are both formless, they are in essence One, not two. There can be no Existence without Consciousness, and no Consciousness without Existence. As pure Existence-Consciousness, śakti is Absolute and Universal. As icchā śakti and kriya śakti and through the various stages of manifestation, She appears as though relative and particular.

These particulars, the various elements or aspects of the phenomenal world, are called tattva-s. According to the Shaiva/ Tantric philosophy, there are 36 tattva-s. Except for śiva tattva, which is the Absolute Consciousness, the other tattva-s are particulars. Since śakti is not separate from Consciousness, śakti is also of śiva tattva. Hence, She is *tattvādhikā,* the one who transcends all tattva-s.

In addition to being known as *tattvādhikā* (the one who transcends), She is also known as *tattvamayī* (the one who is immanent). *Tattvamayī* means that which is immanent in the 36 tattvas. That means śakti pervades as well as transcends the basic elements that constitute the universe. When we recognize the śiva tattva (Consciousness) in every aspect of manifestation, we realize that śakti and śiva are not different. When we closely examine any name, form, or function, from the subtlest (śiva tattva*)* to the grossest (earth/bhūtatva) element, we find that it is pervaded by śakti in the form of Existence-Consciousness, sat-cit. An object IS (*sat*) and we are aware (*cit*) of its existence. We don't think that it does not exist. Although objects appear with particular names, forms, and functions, these particulars cannot transcend *sat-cit. Sat-cit* pervade every object uniformly. It is the substratum on which all objects appear. If an object loses touch with *sat-cit*, it ceases to exist.

That is the reason why Devī, the material cause of this entire universe, is called *tattvamayī.* The mantra *hiranmayi*, also implies the same. Gold is not different from the gold ornaments. Similarly, śakti (*tattvamayi*) is not different from the tattva-s it manifests. Therefore, we must reflect on all the nāma-s that describe the nature of śakti as describing Her expansion (vibhūti), the manifestation of Consciousness into names and forms.

The nāma *tattvādhikā* presents the Goddess as the efficient cause. In the empirical world, an efficient cause is usually separate from the material cause. For instance, the potter (efficient cause) is separate from the clay (the material cause of the pot). The nāma *tattvamayi*, however, presents the Goddess as the material cause. Like the gold that is not different from the ornament, śakti is not different from Her creation. Hence, She is immanent in Her creation as well as transcends it. Since She is both the material and efficient cause, She is *jagadātmaka* (She who pervades the entire world) and *jaganiyāmaka* (She who appointed Herself to transform into the world.). This means everything in this world is Her and by Her divine will. The individual (jīvā), who is a mere notion, is not responsible for anything. He is neither the doer nor the enjoyer. When such an insight into the nature of Devī develops into a firm conviction, the jīvā will be free of saṃsāra.

22. charāchara jagannātha

She who is the ruler of the animate and inanimate worlds.

Although śakti permeates everything, from parā to vaikharī, from śiva to the gross world, it is our great misfortune that we fail to perceive Her. Even though She is the creator and sustainer of the world and we realize we have no control over anything, instead of being detached and peaceful, we are restless and anxious. We transact with the world thinking we are the doers and enjoyers of the results. In reality, we are neither the doers nor the enjoyers. Śakti is the doer of all actions and enjoyer of all results. She is the ruler of all animate and inanimate things (*jagannātha*). The word nātha means "sole refuge." The Supreme Power, parāśakti, is the source and only refuge for all sentient and insentient beings. We must see Her underlying presence (*sat-cit*) in everything, and attribute every action and its results to Her. It is impossible for finite beings like us to interfere in Her process with our limited intellects, since our intellects too conform to Her divine will.

23. sarvānullaṅghya śāsanā

She whose commands are not disobeyed by anyone.

Since She is the commander of all sentient and insentient beings, it is impossible for us to intervene in Her process. No one can transgress Her commands. She reigns over the microcosm and macrocosm with unobstructed power. Everything is in Her control. Every living being abides by Her commands. She is the *kṣetreṣi kṣetrajñapālinī,* the field and the owner of the field as well. Hence, it is not possible for anyone to transcend Her.

Since Devī pervades the insentient world, She has control over everything in the four directions. Everything exists everywhere as She wills. It is impossible for a thing to exist in any other way. Such absolute control is possible because of Her omniscience and omnipresence. It is impossible not only for humans to transcend the boundaries She has drawn for them, but also for all the gods and goddess they worship. According to the Upanishad, it is out of fear of the mahāśakti that the wind blows and the sun shines. When the deities governing the five elements have no control, what control can we ordinary mortals claim? Therefore, we must let go off all doer-ship and surrender ourselves to śakti, the great power that is the source from which the world emanates.

24. pañchakṛtya parāyaṇā

She who is devoted to the five functions.

This nāma describes how the Goddess controls the universe by performing five functions – creation, preservation, destruction, annihilation (tirodhānam), and restoration (anugraham). She performs these functions as She manifests from parā to vaikharī, from Pure Consciousness to the gross world.

Creation, preservation, and dissolution reveal Devī's all-pervasive nature (jagadātmika). This entire phenomenal world emanates from Her, hence it is not different from Her. Her powers of tirodhānam and anugraham, annihilation and restoration, reveal Devī's controlling nature (jaganiyātmika). By contracting Her Infinite Power, She manifest as countless finite beings. By concealing Her real nature, She makes them forget their real nature and live in ignorance. This concealment and resulting ignorance is tirodhānam. By revealing Her true nature, Devī removes ignorance and helps us realize our full potential as siva. This revelation is Her blessing (anugraham). Devī does not perform tirodhānam and anugraham in a random or unchecked manner. She does so in accordance with the merits and demerits accrued by individuals based on their past actions. Pure and Perfect, She is not subject to likes and dislikes.

Although the five functions are attributed to Devī, in reality, they can be reduced to two: tirodhāna and anugraha. Creation, sustenance, and dissolution are part of annihilation, and not apart from it. Because our real nature as Pure Consciousness is concealed from us, we assume that the world is real, that it is created, sustained, and dissolved by some external power. If there was no concealment (tirodhāna), there would be no need for revelation (anugraha). If there was no annihilation, nothing new can be created (śruṣṭi), sustained (sthiti), or dissolved (laya). Consciousness (śakti) would remain Complete and Perfect without any transformation.

25. sṛṣṭikartrī, brahmarūpā; 26. gōptrī, gōvindarūpiṇī; 27. saṃhāriṇī, rudrarūpā; 28. tirōdhānakarī, īśvarī; 29. sadāśivā, ānugrahadā

She who is the Creator - She who is in the form of brahman.
She who protects - She who assumed the form of Govinda (Viṣṇu) for the preservation of the universe.
She who is the destroyer of the universe – She who assumed the form of Rudra for the dissolution of the world.
She who causes the disappearance of all things – She who protects and rules everything.
She who is sadāśivā, one who bestows auspiciousness – She who confers blessings.

These nāma-s describe in detail the manner in which śakti carries out the five functions. First, as brahman (Supreme Consciousness), She manifests this entire universe of sentient and insentient objects. The word brahman stems from the root word bṛhad, which means vast. Devī is *brahmarūpini*, the Supreme Consciousness. There is no difference between śakti and brahman. During the process of manifestation, śakti, the conscious power of brahman, appears as though split into many to appear as this world. Like the gold that molds itself into different ornaments, parā śakti (the great cosmic power) in the form of brahman molded Itself to appear as the world. Although we say "split," in reality, there is no split. The great cosmic power, parāśakti, cannot be fragmented. It only appears as though It is fragmented when It appears as the myriad objects of the world. The mantra *brahmarūpā* indicates that Devī is the material cause of the universe. The mantra *sṛṣṭikartrī* indicates that She is the efficient cause (Intelligence) of the universe. Hence, śakti is both the creator as well as the creation!

Devī is also the sustainer and sustenance of the universe. The names *gōptrī, gōvindarūpiṇī* describes Her role in the universe. As govinda, She rules the world. The syllable "go" also means vṛtti, thought-modifications triggered by the mind and sense organs. As the controller of the mind and the senses, Devī is the ruler and sustainer of the world.

Similarly, as rudra, She withdraws the universe that She has spontaneously created from Herself into Herself. Everything dissolves in Her. Hence, at the time of pralaya (complete dissolution of the world), it is said that the world is not completely destroyed. It becomes un-manifest and merges back into its source (śakti). This is the meaning of *saṃhāriṇī, rudrarūpā*. When śakti manifests externally, we call it creation; when she un-manifests, we call it dissolution. What is real (Consciousness) does not disappear suddenly, and what is unreal (names and forms), does not appear suddenly. This is the fundamental principle of Advaita. The Sanskrit word rudra in this context means primordial sound, the anāhata nāda, the inner vibration. This vibration is the movement of prāṇa, the life-force. At the time of dissolution, this life-force leaves the micro and macrocosm, and merges back into the source, that is citśakti (Consciousness). That is why prāṇa is referred to as rudra. Hence, it is citśakti Itself that manifests as the life-force at the time of creation, and un-manifests and merges back into its source at the time of dissolution.

In this manner, while performing these three functions (creation/sustenance/dissolution), parāśakti conceals Her Infinite nature as citśakti and contracts Herself to appear as the finite world. In this state, She is called Īśvarī, the one who commands, controls, and rules everything. Because of Her controlling and contracting power, we forget our real nature which is Pure Consciousness. Devī also has the power to withdraw and dissolve the world in Herself and reveal Her Infinite nature. She can bestow the Knowledge of the Self and remove the ignorance of an earnest seeker. She can contract Herself to appear as the finite individual or expand freely without any constraint to appear as the Universal Consciousness. In Her ability to contract or expand at will, She is known as *sadāśivā*, the Auspicious One. She pervades the entire universe as Consciousness, so there is really nothing in the Universe that is inauspicious. What appears as saṃsāra is only an appearance of Consciousness. Since Consciousness is ever present, It is *sadāśivā*.

This *sadāśivā* is the fifth stage in the transformation of śakti. This is Her natural state. The four stages we mentioned earlier are only pratiti siddham, only an appearance. They have no reality. Therefore, whatever we perceive as the world is unreal. Consciousness alone is Real. Unable to experience our Self in its full potential as Pure Consciousness, we reduce It to our body, mind, and senses. Identified with the body, we see the world as prakṛti (nature) that is subject to decay and death. We forget our true changeless nature and remain ensnared in the illusion of saṃsāra.

30. viśvarūpā, jāgariṇī; 31. svapantī, taijasātmikā; 32. suptā, prājñātmikā; 33. turyā, sarvāvasthā vivarjitā

She who has the whole universe as her form – She who assumes the form of jīvā in the waking state.
She who assumes the form of the jīvā in the dream state – She who is the inner essence of the jīvā in the dream state.
She who assumes the form of the jīvā in deep sleep state – She who is not separate from prajña.
She who is in the state of turīya – She who transcends all states.

For as long as we forget our true nature and consider ourselves and the world to be finite and separate, in accordance with our outlook, the Goddess projects Herself as the finite world and individual, the macrocosm and the microcosm respectively. This leads to saṃsāra, the cycle of birth and death. The fragment of Consciousness that is attached to the body is the jīvā, the notion of an individual, a separate self. Attached to the individual are three states - the waking, dream, and deep sleep. Identified with these states, the jīvā forgets that he is the witness to these states. In the waking state, he is called viṣva (the self that is identified with the gross body). In the dream state, he is called taijasa (the self that functions as light), and in deep sleep state, he is called prajña (the self that is a witness to the nescience in deep sleep).

It is only a misconception, this notion that the individual experiences three states. In reality, he does not experience any of these states himself. It is Devī, the witnessing Self that is enshrined in him as his innermost Self, that experiences them. She is the one who assumes the form and role of viṣva in the waking state, taijasa in the dream state, and prajña in deep sleep. Since Devī is his innermost Self, jīvā is none other than Her.

If the jīvā is the Devī Herself, then the question arises – is it Devī that is trapped in saṃsāra? Devī is *sarvāvasthā vivarjitā*, the one who transcends all states. Although She is present in all these states, She is not attached to any of them. She is untouched and separate from them as the Consciousness that pervades them. She is not limited by time, space, or events, since time, space, and events are contained in Her. She is turīya, the fourth state that is immanent in all three states as well as transcends them.

In reality, It cannot be called turīya, the fourth state, either. Only when three are really present, there is scope for a fourth. The waking, dream, and deep sleep states don't really exist on their own. They have no existence separate from Consciousness. They appear as though they are separate and real, but they are mithyā, only illusory appearances. If the three states are mere illusions, then why is turīya called the fourth state? The four states are provisionally stated because it is a common misconception that the three states are real, that they are wrought with suffering, and that one must free oneself from suffering by attaining the fourth, turīya. We do not realize that the so called four states are in reality only one, turīya, a state that is not a state, since It is the underlying reality that does not undergo any change. As long as we do not realize the truth that Consciousness (turīya) alone is real, and instead identify as the jīvā and consider the waking, dream, and deep-sleep states as real, Devī will continue to bind us with the noose called tirodhāna and keep us in bondage.

34. bhavachakra pravartinī

She who keeps the wheel of birth and death rotating.

The word *bhava* in this nāma means birth or saṃsāra. Saṃsāra is the wheel of worldly existence that rotates endlessly. This empirical world is called saṃsāra because the jīvā thinks it is helplessly trapped in the endless cycle of birth and death.

In reality, there is no wheel called saṃsāra. It is parāśakti, the Supreme Power, that creates the illusion of a jagat and jīvā. She plays this game in two ways. As *jagadātmika*, She is the wheel of saṃsāra. As *jaganniyāmika*, She is the one who keeps the wheel turning. Therefore, Devī is both the operator and the operation of the world.

What is really present is parāśakti alone. Incapable of grasping the truth that Devī Herself is appearing as saṃsāra, we imagine that saṃsāra is real and that Devī keeps the wheel of saṃsāra rotating. Conforming to the our limited understanding, Devī conceals Her true nature and continues to appear as saṃsāra.

35. sudhāsāgara madhyasthā; 36. kadamba vanavāsinī

She who resides in the center of the ocean of nectar.
She who resides in the kadamba forest.

This nāma describes how Devī appears to the individual. She appears as sudhāsāgara, an ocean of nectar. This ocean is saṃsāra, the phenomenal world that we experience with our mind and sense organs. Since we desire to enjoy the world and everything it offers, saṃsāra appears like nectar. In reality, however, saṃsāra is poison.

Even though the world appears like nectar sometimes, sooner or later, it will reveal its true nature as poison. Nectar and poison represent the pleasures and pains of the world. Devī is the bindu, the point between pleasure and pain. Untouched by either pleasure or pain, She remains in Her intrinsic nature as Universal Consciousness. Although She is not affected by pleasure and pain, She can appear to inflict them on us. In ignorance, instead of recognizing Her as the Universal Consciousness, we imagine there is a saṃsāra and drown in it, tossed around by our likes and dislikes, pains and pleasures.

Saṃsāra is not the end of Devī's journey. She created the kadamba forest in the midst of it. Strong impressions called vāsanā-s, accumulated over life-times, are like the trees in the dense forest. Desires and intentions are like the forest that gives shelter to the trees (vāsanā-s). The kadamba tree is known for its sweet scent. Like the haunting scent of the kadamba tree, these vāsanā-s persist life after life.

37. kularūpiṇī

She who is the deity of the kaula path.
She who is the personification of culture.

This nāma describes how captivated we are by the kadamba forest. The word *kula* here refers to the body made up of five elements – space, wind, water, fire, and earth. These five elements manifest from the three guṇa-s or qualities that make up prakṛti (nature) - ṣatva, rajas, and tamas. The mind is made up of ṣatva. The body and life-force are made up of tamas and rajas respectively. Since the body is a combination of these three guṇa-s, tāntrik*s* refer to the body as *kula*.

Since body is a part of nature, it is subject to the laws of nature. But the jīvā who entered the body is not controlled by nature, since its essential nature is Consciousness. The gross elements have no control over Consciousness. Although its true nature is Consciousness, the jīvā does not realize that. Due to strong tendencies accumulated over lifetimes, it identifies with the body and mind and reduces itself to a finite being. It is this attachment to the body that distances the individual from Devī, the Universal Consciousness. It is this attachment that also keeps the individual imprisoned in his body like a bird in a cage.

38. tvaksthā; 39. rudhira; 40. māṃsaniṣṭhā; saṃsthitā'; 41. mēdōniṣṭhā; 42. asti saṃsthita; 43. majjāsaṃsthā; 44. śukla saṃsthitā

She who lives in the sensibility of the skin.
She who presides over the blood in living beings.
She who presides over the flesh in living beings.

She who resides in the fat of living beings.
She who resides in the bones of living beings.
She who is the presiding deity of the marrow in the bones.
She who resides in the semen.

In addition to holding us captive in the body, Devī surrounds us in the form of the seven dhātu-s, the seven basic building blocks that keep the body functioning – blood, flesh, fat, bones, marrow, and semen. These dhātu-s are the pillars that support the body and prevent it from collapsing. They not only support the external body but also penetrate deep into the core of the body and never forsake it.

We are quite aware of the five dhātu-s - skin, blood, flesh, fat, and bone. We are less aware of the two dhātu-s, majjā (marrow) and śukla (semen). Majjā is the oil-like substance inside the bones, while śukla is the seed that appears white in a man's body. These two dhātu-s nourish and sustain the human body.

The seven dhātu-s are not different from parāśakti. Although they appear as parts of the body, they are a manifestation of śakti. Śakti pervades the entire body, from the skin to the semen. Its form and function are beyond the comprehension of the human mind. Just because the nāma-s says śakti resides or presides over the dhātu-s, we must not make the mistake of thinking that śakti is different from the dhātu-s, or that the dhātu-s exist separately and śakti "entered" them. The dhātu itself is śakti and śakti itself is dhātu. Śakti transforms Herself into the dhātu and pervades (enters) it. She is both their support and content. Visualizing Her as both the support and the content of the body will help strengthen our knowledge and understanding of Devī as the non-dual, all-pervading substance. Therefore, this assemblage of skin, flesh, blood, bone, etc. that we call body is nothing but śakti Herself manifesting in these forms.

45. sumēru madhyaśṛṅgasthā 47. chintāmaṇi gṛhāntasthā

She who sits on the middle peak of Mount Sumeru.
She who sits in the house built of chintāmaṇi. (the wish-full-filling gem).

Devī not only appears as the skin, semen, etc. in our body, She also ascends Mount Sumeru and stations Herself in the middle peak called merudaṇḍa or brahmadaṇḍa. This mountain is not visible externally. It is inside the body, in the middle of the spinal cord that stretches from the bottom of the spine (mūlādhāra) to the crown of the head (sahasrāra). It is the foundational pillar that supports the entire structure of the human body. If the pillar is damaged, the body will no longer function as it should.

On the left and right side of the brahmadaṇḍa (spinal cord) are two nāḍī-s (channels) called ida and piṅgala through which śakti flows upwards. In the center, between these two, is the suṣumṇā nāḍī, which also flows upwards. Yogis call this energy kundalini (coiled female serpent) because, like a serpent that uncoils itself and crawls out of its nest and rests in a cave, suṣumṇā nāḍī starts from the root chakra and crawls upwards to the crown chakra and rests there.

The seeker who recognizes this upward movement of the śakti will realize his true nature and be liberated. This upward movement of śakti manifests in the seeker as the desire to know the Self (Self-inquiry) and the recognition of the Self. To liberate the seeker, śakti enters the cave of his intellect in the form of Self-Knowledge and waits for his realization. That cave or intellect is the house of *chintāmaṇi*. Chintā refers to the activity of the mind and intellect. The ongoing flow of thoughts are like a string of gem stones (maṇi).

The mind is like an ocean, and the thoughts that arise from in it are like the waves in the ocean. Repetitive thoughts harden into tendencies (vāsanā-s). Like the lingering scent of the kadamba tree, these tendencies cling to the tree called the body. Devī pervades this entire tree, from its roots to its crown. She is *chintāmaṇi*, the supreme intelligence that resides in our intellect, that can free us from vāsanā-s and liberate us. Hence, Devī is both the means and the end. There is nothing outside Her power.

47. jñānavigrahā 48. ātmā

She who is the embodiment of Knowledge.
She who is the Self in all.

Hence, śakti manifests as the conglomeration of different parts that we call our body. We perceive the body as an object. An object is that which is known to a knower. In reality, however, the body is not an object. It is Knowledge itself! When everything is pervaded by Devī, who is pure Knowledge or Awareness, how can there be forms or objects that are separate from Her? If She has a form, that form can only be Awareness. A form that is not a form. Awareness is formless. Awareness pervades the entire body and mind. If there is no touch of Awareness, there is no experience. If a thorn is stuck in our foot, we feel the pain all the way in our head. It does not stop at our foot. Without Awareness, we would not even be aware or experience the fact that we have a foot. Without Awareness, we would not be aware of the world outside. Because our Awareness expands and pervades the Sun, we are aware of the Sun. Therefore, for an object to exist or for us to know that it exists, Consciousness must first be present.

Another name for this Knowledge, Awareness, or Consciousness is ātmā. That which is expansive is ātmā. Ātmā pervades the entire world (objects), cognizes the world as the Self (subject), dissolves the world completely in Itself, and continues in its formless nature as the Universal Consciousness. Therefore, ātmā is the object (known), the subject (knower of the object), and the Self in all. It is the experience or awareness that "I Am." Just as It is aware of Its own existence (Self), ātmā is also aware of the existence of the world (not Self). All experiences in essence are of the same nature, whether it is the experience of the Self or of the world. Experience is Knowledge. Knowledge is the same regardless of its content.

49. ābālagōpa viditā

She who is well known to all, from a child to a cowherd.

We have so far discussed the nature of ātmā and concluded that everything we perceive is of the nature of ātmā. Ātmā is not like an object that is out of reach. It is the substance that is directly known and experienced by everyone equally, from the least intelligent (bāla) to the most intelligent (gōpa).

How do we know for a fact that ātmā is experienced equally by everyone? When someone asks us, "who are you?," our answer invariably starts with "I Am..." We do not distance ourselves from our Self by saying "I am not..." Because we intuitively are aware of our own Self, we utter the words "I Am…" spontaneously. This intuitive I-Am-ness or Self-awareness is ātmā. It is experienced equally by everyone, from an innocent child to a learned scholar. However, although ātmā is our very nature, we do not perceive It because we identify with particulars, such as the body, life-force, and mind, and not with the underlying Consciousness in which they appear. We consider the world real and engage with it with a sense of doer-ship and enjoyer-ship. We totally identify with the objects we perceive and fail to separate ourselves from them. We do not realize that we are the Consciousness in which the objects appear and disappear.

When we stop identifying with the world (anātmā) and perceive everything as the Self (ātmā), when there is nothing left to bind us, we will be free of saṃsāra. Even a learned scholar is as good as an ignorant person, if he sees the world and himself as separate entities. Only the one who realizes the Self and sees the Self in All is the Accomplished one (paṇḍita). Expertise in a particular field of knowledge does not make one a paṇḍita. As long as one sees duality - me and mine, Self and not-self, one remains in ignorance. He is the Self, but not the knower of the Self.

50. manōrūpēkṣukōdaṇḍā; 51. pañchatanmātra sāyakā; 52. rāgasvarūpa pāśāḍhyā; 53. krōdhākārāṅkuśōjjvalā

She who holds in Her hand a sugarcane bow that represents the mind.
She who holds the five subtle elements as arrows (touch, smell, hearing, taste, and, sight).
She who holds the rope of love in Her hand.
She who shines bearing the goad of anger.

Because of our dualist minds, we do not recognize the non-dual Self or ātmā that is ever present and shining in our body as the Universal Self that pervades everything. Instead of a homogenous vision that sees the universal, we have a heterogenous vision that sees particulars. Mind is a fragment of the Universal Consciousness. Although it is of the nature of Consciousness, it is not complete or universal because it is fragmented by vṛtti-s or thought-modifications. Like waves in an ocean, thoughts rise and subside in the mind endlessly, creating a fragmented vision.

Supreme Consciousness has entered and stationed Itself in the mind. The mind has been described earlier as chintāmaṇi, the jewel of Consciousness. Although Devī pervades everything, Her presence is felt most strongly in the mind or the intellect. However, only one in a million of seekers realize this. Even though the mind is our only means to realize the Truth, instead of using it for that purpose, we foolishly squander it on pleasures. To remind us about the nature of the mind, Devī holds a sugarcane bow in Her hand. The juice in the sugarcane is pleasure. But the cane is destructive. Like the sweetness that pervades every drop of the juice, thoughts pervade the mind. The more we extract and enjoy the sweetness of the sugarcane, the more our desire for it grows. Similarly, the more we indulge our mind and senses in pleasures, the more our desire grows. Desire and greed only increase if we keep trying to satisfy our mind and senses. That is why the mind is compared to a sugarcane.

Devī holds the mind like a bow in Her hand. The mind that seeks pleasure is the sugarcane bow in Her hands. Although it appears like a source of pleasure, the bow is a destructive weapon. Devi strings the bow with arrows and shoots them one after the other. These arrows are the five senses called the tanmātra-s – touch, smell, sound, form, and taste. Like arrows, they enter the mind through the senses organs and generate sensuous thoughts and feelings. Persisting thoughts, sensations, and emotions become strong tendencies (vāsanā-s) that give way to for even more stronger thoughts, sensations, and emotions. Devī strings the bow called the mind and shoots the arrows called thoughts and emotions. This is a vicious cycle. The mind is constantly pulled in multiple directions by the sense organs, which are also weapons in the hands of Devī.

Besides the bow, Devī holds two other weapons in Her hand – a rope (pāśaṃ) and a hook (aṅkuśam). The rope stands for desires (likes) and the hook stands for anger (dislikes). Devī binds us with the rope and pierces us with the hook. Likes and dislikes are the cause for the pleasures and pains we experience in life.

These four nāma-s clearly describe what bondage is. Desires activate the senses. Senses activate the mind. The activated mind turns towards objects to satisfy the desires. If the results of its actions are satisfactory, it experiences pleasure. If they are not satisfactory, it experiences pain. Hence, likes and dislikes are bondage.

What do the tools that Devī holds in Her four hands signify? That the mind and sense organs, likes and dislikes, are in the hands of Devī. We have no control over them. Because we lack the knowledge of the Self, we are born as prisoners and continue to live as prisoners of our mind and sense organs. As long as we are ignorant (lack the Knowledge of the Self), Devī will continue to shoot Her arrows at us. If we pray to Her in earnest to rid us of the disease called ignorance, She will withdraw Her weapons and bestow Knowledge. She can free us from saṃsāra or entrench us deeply in it. It is to reveal the truth that Knowledge alone can free us from saṃsāra that Devī is described as holding four powerful weapons in Her hands.

54. sarvamōhinī

She who deludes all.

Those who do not realize the truth and fail to grasp Devī as their own Self will continue to remain in deep slumber, steeped in ignorance. In spite of attaining a human birth, they will live meaningless lives like animals. They will make no effort whatsoever to understand the nature of the world and transcend it. The great enchantress, mahāmāyā, will continue to tempt and drown such people in the ocean of desires. She is after all *sarvamōhinī*, the one who deludes all. Her very nature is to enchant and delude the ignorant. Since almost every human being on earth is deluded by the world and lives in ignorance, Devī is verily called *sarvamōhinī.*

Summary

In the 54 nāma-*s* we discussed so far, from the first nāma (*śri māta*) to the last nāma *(sarvamōhinī*), we have discussed the descent of the Goddess from the un-manifest to the manifest. As *mahāśakti*, She is the creator-sustainer-destroyer of the universe. As *jaganmāta*, She is the Divine Mother who nourishes the Universe. How can such a mother willfully drown Her children in the ocean of saṃsāra*?* Shouldn't a mother have only love and compassion, for her children? It is natural for one to wonder why the Divine Mother operates in such a seemingly partial manner towards Her creation. We answered this question earlier. But let us discuss it in more detail now.

There is no doubt that Devi is the Divine Mother. Because She is the mother, She does not willfully throw us into the ocean of saṃsāra. In reality, She does not move from Her natural state as Pure Consciousness at all. That there is a world is only a notion imagined by the ignorant mind. Due to avidyā (nescience), we have forgotten the real nature of our Self, which is undifferentiated Pure Consciousness. Instead, we have divided it into two fragments, the finite self (jīvā) and the world (jagat). Because of this fragmented view of the Self, we are subject to three afflictions - physical, environmental, and karmic. We ascribe our suffering to the tirodhāna śakti or the concealing power of Devī.

The truth is Devī never really concealed Herself from us. Since She is Consciousness Itself, She is shining everywhere as Existence-Consciousness (sat-cit). Whatever we perceive, jīvā or jagat, we are aware of its existence (Beingness). Without any distinction, whether it is "me or "mine," everything presents itself as sat-cit, Existence-Consciousness. Since She shines as presence everywhere, how can Devī conceal Her true nature? It is our own limited mind and intellect that fail to recognize Her.

Hence, it is only a misconception produced by a faulty vision that makes us think Devī descended from Her abode, created this world, and trapped us helplessly in it. In reality, however, neither did She descend into the world nor did She trap us in it. These are mere notions, imagination, and not the Absolute Truth. We cannot ascribe descent or delusion to the Goddess. The problem is the jīvā, the notional separate-self, born out of ignorance that drowns itself in an imagined saṃsāra and erroneously ascribes its plight to the Goddess.

Hence, we are to blame ourselves, and not the Divine Mother for our suffering. It is our ignorance, our inability to recognize the divine nature of our own Self that is the problem. It is ignorance that keeps us separate and away from our true Self, which is Devī Herself. That separation, the distancing of ourselves from our source, is the descent (avarohaṇa) of Devi. The moment Knowledge arises and ignorance is removed, we will find ourselves back in the lap of the Divine Mother. This realization or knowledge of the Self is the ascent (ārohaṇa). The ascent and descent of the Goddess must be understood as the ascent and descent of the jīvā.

We have now completed the study of the nāma-s that describe the descent of Devī. In the next chapter, we will study the 54 nāma-s that describe Her ascent.

CHAPTER 2

The Ascent

In this chapter, the ascent of the Goddess from the manifest to the un-manifest Pure Consciousness is described in 54 nāma-s or mantras. The table below lists the nāma-s and their approximate location in the original sahasranāma (1000 names of the Goddess).

#	Divine Name (nāma)	No.	#	Divine Name (nāma)	No.
1	avyāja karuṇāmūrti	992	28	nirbhēdā	178
2	dēvakāryasamudyatā	5	29	bhēdanāśinī	179
3	śivadūtī	408	30	nirmamā	164
4	gurumūrti	603	31	nirahaṅkārā	161
5	śāstrasārā	845	32	mṛtyumathanī	181
6	śivajñāna pradāyinī	727	33	nirbhavā	174
7	paśupāśa vimōchanī	354	34	śāntā	141
8	muktidā	736	35	brāhmī	675
9	bahirmukha sudurlabhā	871	36	parāniṣṭhā	573
10	antarmukha samārādhyā	870	37	hēyōpādēya varjitā	304
11	mithyā jagadadhiṣṭhānā	735	38	abhyāsātiśaya jñātā	990
12	vidyā'vidyā svarūpiṇī	402	39	maitryādi vāsanālabhyā	570
13	duṣṭadūrā	193	40	ajñānadhvānta dīpikā	993
14	śiṣṭēṣṭā	411	41	jñānajñēya svarūpiṇī	981
15	saṃhṛtāśēṣa pāṣaṇḍā	355	42	sāmarasya parāyaṇā	792
16	sadāchāra pravartikā	356	43	svasthā	914
17	samayāchāra tatparā	98	44	ēkākinī	665
18	sampradāyēśvarī	710	45	duḥkhahantrī	191

#	Divine Name (nāma)	No.	#	Divine Name (nāma)	No.
19	mahāvidyā	584	46	puruṣārthapradā	291
20	brahmātmāikya svarūpiṇī	672	47	svargāpavargadā	764
21	tattvamartha svarūpiṇī	908	48	nirvāṇa sukhadāyinī	390
22	vimarṣarūpiṇī	548	49	sadyaḥ prasādinī	383
23	parāparā	790	50	yajamāna svarūpiṇī	883
24	prasiddhā	395	51	sarvāntaryāminī	819
25	bhāvanāgamyā	113	52	pūrṇā	292
26	dhyānagamyā	641	53	śāśvatī	951
27	dhyānadhyātṛ dhyēyarūpā	254	54	śrī śivā	998

1. avyāja karuṇāmūrti

She who is pure compassion.

Devī is the embodiment of compassion. As the Mother of the Universe, She only has compassion for Her children. She shares Her wealth generously and equally with all. Existence-Consciousness (satta-spuratta) are Her wealth. We perceive them everywhere, not only as the substratum on which particulars appear, but also as the particulars themselves. Just as we experience our spouse, children, possessions, etc. externally, we experience pleasures and pains internally. Devī shares Her wealth in these two ways with Her children, as the external world of objects and the internal world of thoughts, perceptions, and emotions. Her love flows unconditionally and profusely towards all.

If there is any dearth, it is in our perception. We have forgotten the compassionate One who is the source of our very existence. We are not satisfied with what She offers. We want more and chase after our desires. We run after objects and completely overlook Her presence, the underlying reality of all the objects we desire. In our ignorance, instead of recognizing what is as Her grace, we consider it an affliction (saṃsāra). Only those who contemplate on Her true nature relentlessly and yearn to realize Her are worthy of Her grace. She floods them with Her love and compassion. To such earnest seekers, who are free from the darkness of desire and attachment, She is no longer *mohini*, the one who enchants and distracts them from the truth. She is *anugrāhini*, the one who reveals the truth. In the light of the Self-Knowledge Devī bestows on them, these seekers no longer perceive names and forms. Instead, they perceive Devī everywhere as sat-cit, Presence-Awareness. While the rest of the world is asleep in ignorance, they remain awake in Self-Knowledge.

2. dēvakāryasamudyatā

She who is intent on fulfilling the wishes of the gods.

This nāma describes the nature of those who are favored by Devī. The word *deva* in this nāma does not refer to celestial gods (devatā-s) residing in heaven. It refers to seekers who are endowed with divine qualities. Even if they reside in heaven, if the deva-s do not have the necessary divine qualities, they do not qualify for Her grace.

Those who have essential qualities like śraddhā, utmost faith and perseverance, are the real devatā-s. The actions of such divine beings are divine actions. Since their only desire is for truth and liberation from the cycle of birth and death. Devī frees such them from the ocean of saṃsāra. She never ignores them. The harder they strive for truth, the more benevolent She is towards them. Since they seek Her to realize the Truth, She reveals Her true nature to them.

3. śivadūtī

She who is siva's messenger.

Those who strive for Self-Knowledge are true seekers. Devī's job is to liberate them. Although She is *śivakāmēśvarāṅkasthā* (the one who sits in the lap of śiva; She who is the conqueror of desire), She descends into the world like a messenger of śiva to free them. That is why she is called *śivadūtī*, the one who is the messenger of śiva.

A messenger's job is to convey the message. The sender of the message is paramātma, the Supreme Consciousness. Since the sender is Pure Consciousness, immutable, changeless, and motionless, It cannot go anywhere. Hence, Devī, kriyā śakti (the power to act), is his messenger. She can appear in an instant anywhere and everywhere. He is like the sun that remains still in space, and She is like the sun rays that spread across the entire universe. Devī permeates everything as *sat-cit*. As the messenger of śiva, She reveals the Supreme Knowledge of the Self to earnest seekers of truth.

4. gurumūrti

She who has assumed the form of the guru.

How do we know that Devī descended into the world as the messenger of śiva? This nāma answers this question. Devī descends into the world in the form of a Guru. She is not visible to us in Her real form, since she is śakti (power/energy). Śakti in Her pure form cannot be perceived. Therefore, She appears to us in the form of an ācārya, teacher of Self-Knowledge. There is no difference between Devī and an ācārya. This is the meaning of the verse *guru sākṣāt parambrahma* (guru is the Supreme Consciousness Itself).

The formless appears in the form of a guru to uplift seekers who sincerely strive for Self-Knowledge. As the seeker gains Self-Knowledge and establishes in It, Devī frees him or her from the bondage of saṃsāra. It is our duty to seek and serve such teachers. Only with their blessing and guidance, we can attain our goal. When our efforts bear fruit, it means Devī 's effort has borne fruit.

5. śāstrasārā

She who is the essence of all scriptures.

This nāma explains how a Guru teaches and enlightens a disciple. The teaching must be based on valid evidence (pramāṇa). Bhagavad Gita declares the scripture (Upanishads) as the pramāṇa, a valid means of Knowledge. Without pramāṇa, the prameya (object of knowledge) cannot be grasped. The "object" in Advaita is the sarvātmābhava, the intuitive knowledge that "I am the Self in All." Such knowledge is attained only through the scripture, and not through direct perception or inference. Direct perception and inference work in anātmā (object world), and not in ātmā. Hence, scripture is the only means of Knowledge about ātmā.

How can ātmā become the object of knowledge for the scripture? Isn't ātmā aprameya, that which cannot be known as an object (prameya) through any pramāṇa? Yes, it is true that ātmā is ever the subject that knows, and never the object that is known. Even the scripture does not treat ātmā as an object. The scripture (Upanishads) provides us with the knowledge of the Self by negating everything that appears as an object to It. This is the methodology adapted by the scripture. It takes a negative approach, not a positive approach, to prove the existence of ātmā. Therefore, even if we say ātmā is the object of knowledge for the scripture, there is no problem, since the scripture does not directly describe the ātmā, rather its methodology is to refute everything that is not ātmā. The knowledge of the Self is obtained only through the teacher-disciple tradition using scripture as the means. Scripture is like a bridge between the teacher and the student. A teacher is one who is knowledgeable and capable of teaching others. Scripture is the only medium through which the Knowledge of ātmā can be transmitted. For the teacher, Knowledge is in the form of experience (Self-realization). For the student, Knowledge is in the form of receiving (listening) and contemplating on the teaching.

6. śivajñāna pradāyinī

She who bestows the knowledge of śiva.

It is said that the scripture is the only source of jñāna or Self-Knowledge. But the scripture expounds on dharma (virtuous actions) as well as jñāna. How can we then say that scripture is the only source of Self-Knowledge?

This nāma answers this question. Knowledge corresponding to śiva, the Supreme Consciousness, is the Knowledge of the Self. Since Devī bestows this Knowledge, She is called *śiva jñāna pradāyini.* Knowledge is of two types: śivam and aśivam. All types of knowledge pertaining to the material world and the actions performed in the material world (dharma*)* are aśivam. They do not help the seeker attain śiva. Even though dharma appears to be superior to other types of knowledge, upon some reflection, it will soon become clear to us that even dharma is not Supreme Knowledge because it produces only temporary results, such as the attainment of svarga (heaven). Hence, even dharma does not liberate us.

When we continue to reflect on the transient nature of the world and realize that all types of knowledge associated with it are aśivam and dismiss them, we are left with what is śivam, the Supreme Knowledge of the Self. Everything that is aśivam (saṃsāra) dissolves in śivam. Knowledge of the Self is the only means for the dissolution of saṃsāra and attainment of śiva. Therefore, the real goal of the scripture is Self-Knowledge. Knowledge of dharma is, at best, only a distant aid (for purification of the mind) to Self-Knowledge. Hence, there is no need to be concerend that the scripture provides conflicting knowledge (jñāna versus dharma).

7. paśupāśa vimōchanī; 8. muktidā

She who liberates the ignorant from bondage.
She who gives liberation.

Devi appears in the form of a Guru to give Self-Knowledge, which is the essence of the scripture. This nāma describes how this Knowledge benefits us. The benefit is *paśupāśa vimōchanī*, freedom from the bondage of ignorance. That which is bound by a pāśaṃ (rope) is a paśu (beast). This includes four-legged and two-legged creatures like animals and humans. Humans are bound by many ropes (kleśa-s) or afflictions: avidyā (ignorance), asmitā (ego), rāga (likes), dveṣa (dislikes), and abhīnavesa (fear of death). These afflictions are the five ropes that bind us in saṃsāra. The first affliction, avidyā, is the lack of knowledge that I and everything I perceive are One (Consciousness). Like a thick curtain, avidyā veils our true nature, which is Pure Consciousness. As a result, we perceive Consciousness as limited to our body. This ignorance leads to asmitā (ego) and the feeling of separateness. This feeling of separateness is the second rope that binds us in saṃsāra.

Likes and dislikes are the two additional ropes that bind us. We are happy when desires are satisfied and miserable when they are not. As long as we are identified with the body, we are subject to likes and dislikes. Obsession with our likes and dislikes strengthens our identification with the body and our fear of death. This is the fifth affliction. Avidyā is tamas (ignorance), asmitā is moham (infatuation), rāga is mahāmoha (attachment), dveṣa is tāmisram (darkness), ad abhīnavesa is andha tāmisram (dense darkness). These five afflictions are the five hells that humans are trapped in. While the first affliction (avidyā) is somewhat visible to us, the last one (abhīnavesa) is completely invisible.

Bound by these five afflictions, the jīva is reduced to a beast. The first affliction, avidyā, is the source of the other afflictions. If avidyā is removed, the rest of the afflictions will fall away on their own. Ātmajñāna (Self-Knowledge) is the only means for getting rid of avidyā. The moment Devī graces the jīva with Self-Knowledge, along with avidyā, the rest of the kleśa-s disappear. The jīva is freed from the beast-like qualities that bind it in saṃsāra.

This freedom is liberation. It is the mokṣa that Devi bestows on us. Hence, Devi is revered as *muktidā,* the one who liberates. Several questions might arise at this point. Is it really possible to attain mokṣa, for instant Knowledge to arise? Isn't Knowledge a vṛtti, a thought-modification, a mental activity? Even if the mind attains Self-Knowledge, can it really dissolve the physical world? Don't we need to make some physical effort to get rid of the world after the Knowledge arises?

There is no scope for such doubts to arise. Knowledge of the Self is not like other types of knowledge. Even if it is a vṛtti, it is not kāṇḍa (divisive) vṛtti. It is the undifferentiated vṛtti of the Infinite Consciousness. It is devoid of all divisions (names and forms). It permeates not only the mind of the seeker, but also everything he or she perceives. Names and forms lose their separate existence. Consciousness alone remains. Names and forms derive their existence from Consciousness, and have no existence of their own. Therefore, the moment the Knowledge of the Self arises, ignorance disappears. Together with ignorance, the world, also disappears. Therefore, no separate effort is required to get rid of the world when Knowledge arises. The instant Knowledge arises, one is free from bondage, and the moment one is free from bondage, one is liberated!

9. bahirmukha sudurlabhā; 10. antarmukha samārādhyā

She who is difficult to attain by those whose attention is directed outwards.
She who is worshipped internally.

As discussed earlier, the instant Self-Knowledge arises, the seeker is automatically freed from bondage. Liberation is Self-Knowledge. There is no difference between them. Self is the ātmā, the intuitive "I Am" awareness that every human being experiences from the time of birth. One cannot deny one's own existence. Since ātmā is our very nature and it is readily available to us at all times, there is no need to make a special effort to attain it.

In the mantra *bahirmukha sudurlabhā*, the word sudurlabhā means that which is difficult to attain. Devī is hard to attain since She is the Knowledge that transcends everything. If She cannot be attained, there is no hope for liberation. Although She is all-pervading, She is difficult to attain. Why? This is because our attention is always flowing outward (*bahirmukha*) and never inwards.

We live our lives obsessed with the external world. Because our attention is always focused on external objects, even though Devī's presence is right here and everywhere, we fail to notice Her. Even if an object is right in front of us, it remains unavailable to us if we fail to notice it. Even if it is very close to us physically, it is as good as being at a great distance if our attention is elsewhere and not on it. Therefore, we end up seeing what we see, but not what is actually present.

In this manner, seeing other things instead of what is actually present is bahirmukha. We see names and forms, build relationships, and suffer pain and pleasure. We perceive objects and completely overlook the substratum on which they appear. The substratum is Devī, Pure Consciousness, that pervades everything. Because our vision fails to grasp Her even though She is present everywhere, She appears difficult to attain. We can only blame our finite mind for this.

How can we solve this problem? How can we attain Her? We can attain Her only if our attention is turned inwards. Attaining Her or worshiping Her means being continuously aware of Her presence (*sat-cit*). When our attention is totally focused on Her presence, we can easily attain Her. Like the objects in a dark room that reveal themselves as soon as a lamp is lit, Devī reveals Herself soon as our attention turns inwards. Therefore, even though it appears as though She is hard to attain, for the one whose attention is turned inwards, She is easy to attain.

The words "inwards" and "outwards" do not mean inside and outside our minds. As long as feelings, such as "this is my son, this is my friend, this is my enemy, etc." arise in our mind, it is outward-facing or bahirmukha. When our attention is on the universal *sat-cit*, Existence-Consciousness, and not on particulars, it is *antarmukha*, inward-facing.

11. mithyā jagadadhiṣṭhānā

She who is the basis of the illusory universe.

How can we cultivate antarmukha, an inward vision? We can do so by contemplating deeply on the nature of Devī, who is the substratum on which the illusory world appears. She is the great power or śakti that is the basis of the entire universe. But we fail to notice Her because our attention is only on the transitory names and forms that are superimposed on it. Names and forms are countless, change endlessly, and produce mixed results. If the results are good, we are happy. If the results are bad, we are unhappy. We have no choice but to helplessly experience the results, good or bad.

This feeling of helplessness is because our attention is on the transient world. Our effort now is to see the world as a superimposition, as a mere appearance. It is only Consciousness that appears as names and forms. It is like the rays of the sun appearing as water (mirage) in the desert. The sun rays are real. Their appearance as water (mirage) is unreal.

Similarly, even if the phenomenal world appears to us, it is like a mirage. It is only a shadow of Pure Consciousness. It is real only as Consciousness, and unreal as names and forms. The more we contemplate on the infinite nature of Consciousness and our minds expand to grasp it, the more illusory the world will appear and disappear altogether eventually. When the entire world disappears, Pure Consciousness alone remains, just like the sun rays that remain when the mirage disappears.

12. vidyā'vidyā svarūpiṇī

She who is in the form of both knowledge and ignorance.

Based on the above discussion, it is clear that we are capable of two visions, one that sees the real substance and the one that sees the unreal appearance. These two viewpoints are valid in the empirical as well as the spiritual realms. Even in the empirical world, if our attention is only on the external appearance of an object and not on its internal nature, we would be seeing only the unreal. Only when our attention penetrates and understands the internal nature of the object, we really see the object in its entirety. These real and unreal viewpoints are vidyā and avidyā respectively. However, from the viewpoint of Supreme Consciousness, even vidyā is avidyā. Mundaka Upanishad declared all vidyā-s (knowledge about particulars), including Rigveda as avidyā. Real Knowledge or vidyā is that which reveals the Absolute truth.

This nāma describes Devī as *vidyā-avidyā swarūpini*. How can Devī, who is Pure Consciousness, be avidyā? Isn't She also vimarṣa-rūpini, the one who is the source of all vidyā-s? Nowhere has Devī been described as avidyā, but in this mantra! What does that mean?

Vidyā-avidyā do not belong to Devī. They belong to the jīvā. If the jīvā's vision is on the real, then Devī appears as vidyā. If it is on the unreal, Devī appears as avidyā. The knowledge of the finite jīvā is limited and unstable. It comes and goes. When vidyā rises, avidyā disappears. When avidyā rises, vidyā disappears. Therefore, the individual's knowledge is not steady. It keeps changing. But the Supreme Knowledge that is Devī does not change.

Why does this nāma describe Her as vidyā-avidyā? How should we interpret it? Vidyā and avidyā are relative terms. Because there is vidyā, there is avidyā. Because there is avidyā, there is vidyā. When the mind ceases to see duality, what remains is Devī in Her essential nature as Consciousness. Devī is described as both vidyā and avidyā because there is nothing outside Her nature. The seeker must dissolve these conflicting notions and feelings, and perceive Devī as the all-pervading Pure Consciousness that ever shines and never sets.

13. duṣṭadūrā; 14. śiṣṭēṣṭā

She who is unapproachable by the wicked
She who is loved by the righteous; She who is the chosen deity; She who loves righteous people.

Those who cannot see Devī as the all-pervading Pure Consciousness are duṣṭa or wicked. Devī remains unreachable and ungraspable by such people. They are regarded as "sinners" because of the three doṣā-s they commit. The first doṣā is avidyā (ignorance), which leads to the second called kāma (desire), which in turn leads to the third called karma (action). Lack of proper knowledge of the Self (ātmā) is avidyā. Due to avidyā, Self appears as the anātmā (the not-self - world, objects, people, relationships, etc.) When anātmā appears, desire arises. This is kāma, desire for worldly pleasures. Kāma produces action (karma) to satisfy the desires. Action (karma) produces results. Results, good or bad, must be experienced. Hence, the source of saṃsāra are these three doṣā-s: avidyā, kāma, and karma.

The extent to which we are subject to these doṣā-s to that extent we are duṣṭa-s. Hence, Devī appears as though out of our reach. In reality, She is right here, but hidden from us. Like three thick curtains, the three doṣā-s hide Her from our view. That is why we cannot grasp Her. Hence, She is called *duṣṭadūrā*, the one who unattainable by duṣṭa-s.

How can we attain Her? How can we get rid of all our desires and dissolve our mind in Her completely? This second nāma, *śiṣṭeṣṭā*, answers this question. We must get rid of these doṣā-s. When these doṣā-s disappear, the duṣṭa transforms into a śiṣṭa, the noble one. Such noble ones are dear to Devī because their only desire is to know the truth. This is a common occurrence – to first desire a thing, then to make an effort to attain it, and finally to make it our own.

For instance, if we desire to eat a particular type of sweet, if our desire is strong enough, we will explore all the ways in which we can quickly acquire the sweet and satisfy our desire. We now have a desire to attain Devī. Although Devī is our very own Self, we have forgotten this truth over several life times. Now that we desire to know Her, we are inspired to seek Her. As our desire becomes stronger, our effort to attain Her also becomes stronger and will eventually culminate in experiencing Her as our own Self. Because She is desired and sought by śiṣṭa-s and She in turn favors them, She is śiṣṭēṣṭā.

Sri Krishna echoes this truth in Bhagavad Gita, Ch 7-17 as follows: "I consider them to be the highest, who worship Me with knowledge, and are steadfastly and exclusively devoted to Me. I am very dear to them and they are very dear to Me."

The desire to attain Devī is not like a desire to attain material objects, such as sweets. In order to satisfy our desire for sweets, we must either make them from scratch or acquire them from a store. No such transactions are necessary in satisfying our desire for Devī. Consciousness pervades everything. It does not have to be newly created or acquired from some distant place. It is readily present as our own Self. All that we need to do is to remove the three doṣā-s that conceal It. We will then experience Devī as our very own Self. This recognition of the divine nature of our Self is pratyabhijñā. Such a recognition is the only effort required by śiṣṭa-s.

15. saṃhṛtāśēṣa pāṣaṇḍā; 16. sadāchāra pravartikā

She who destroys all heretics.
She who is immersed in right conduct and inspires others to follow.

Like the śiṣṭa-s, duṣṭa-s are also created by Devī . How can She be partial to one and not to the other of Her creation? Isn't She karuṇa mūrti, the compassionate one? As the Divine Mother of all, shouldn't She have equanimity towards all?

There is no doubt that Devī treats all Her creation equally. She destroys all heretical doctrines, such as those of the materialists (cārvāka-s) that get popularized in the world from time to time. These doctrines appeal to masses because they are easy to follow. Most humans are of mediocre intelligence. By associating themselves with such heretical doctrines, they become duṣṭa-s. They live in avidyā, obsessed by kāma and karma. They are satisfied with material pleasures, and have no aspiration for higher knowledge. They live in ignorance, die in ignorance, and are reborn in ignorance.

Devī transforms duṣṭa-s into *śiṣṭa*-s by destroying doctrines that distract and mislead them. That is the reason why great teachers (*acārya*-s) appear in certain locations of the world from time to time. It is only due to Devī's grace and the power of Self-Knowledge that She bestows on them that these teachers are able to drive away heretical teachings, and reestablish right thinking and order in the world. Shankara and Ramanuja are such great sages that appeared in the past, and there are many in the present who are also working hard towards spreading the Knowledge that can free people from saṃsāra. The passion and commitment with which these sages accomplish their goals is a manifestation of the power of Devī.

The wise say that one must save oneself first and then save others. These sages have a wealth of Knowledge. They have rid themselves of the three doṣā-s and freed themselves from the clutches of saṃsāra. If we keep company of such wise sages and follow their instructions, we too will be free. People are infatuated by those who have attained name and fame, and follow them without any discrimination. If these famed people propagate wrong teachings, people who follow them will apply the wrong teaching to their lives and become entrenched deeper in the three doṣā-s. If they follow a teacher who propagates sadācāra, the right teaching, they become śiṣṭa-s. Devī gives birth to such wise teachers from time to time to guide seekers to the right path.

17. samayāchāra tatparā; 18. sampradāyēśvarī

She who is attached to the samaya form of worship.
She who is the guardian of traditions.

This nāma describes the nature of sadācāra, the virtuous path that is also known as samayācāra. Sadācāra unites the individual consciousness (jīvātma) with the Supreme Consciousness (paramātmā). Hence it is considered as a virtuous path.

Devī is the essence of sadācāra traditions and not of the opposite path called vāmācāra. There are different traditions and practices for seekers in the world. Vāmācāra, kaulācāra, and dakṣinācāra are the three most popular ones. Vāmācāra is the most intense of the three because it involves extreme practices. Kaulācāra involves rituals and symbolic worship, while dakṣinācāra focuses on Truth. Hence, wise men prefer dakṣinācāra. If they follow this path, they are bound to attain liberation. Liberation is Pure Knowledge. The other practices, vāmācāra *and* kaulācāra, do not help seekers attain the ultimate goal, which is the direct experience of the Self. Only when seekers on these other paths slowly let go of practices that perpetuate differences (multiplicity) and turn instead towards dakṣinācāra, they will attain liberation. Therefore, all traditions eventually must culminate in dakṣinācāra, the path that reveals the Truth.

The sages of the Upanishads unanimously declare sadācāra as the only practice that leads to Pure Knowledge. They established sadācāra as the sampradāya to be followed by everyone in the world. Sampradāya is the tradition by which an enlightened teacher passes on his or her experiential Knowledge to a disciple. It is this teacher-disciple tradition that is popular in the world. Those who have purified their mind by cultivating the six virtues (*sama*, *dama*, etc.) and have developed one-pointed concentration on the truth are qualified for sadācāra. They are sure to reap the rewards of their practice. Those who do not qualify for sadācāra are in capable of grasping the Knowledge, so there is no danger of such people contaminating the teaching.

Several questions may arise at this point. Is śāstra (scripture) the only means of attaining this Knowledge? Can't we attain this Knowledge by observing the world? Our intellect is ever present, so we should be able to grasp anything with our intellect and experience it. Why then are we instructed to learn from a teacher? A teacher might be very knowledgeable and, based on his knowledge, he/she might show us a path. But why should we consider the path they show as the only path? Can't we investigate and find another path using our own intellect? Won't our intellect expand and sharpen if we exercise it in this manner?

Such questions arise due to lack of proper enquiry. Seekers around the world are not all equally competent. They may be grouped into different types based on their competency, such as the brilliant (uttamottama), good (uttama), mediocre (madhyma), and beginner (adhama) types. The brilliant ones are those who do not need the scripture or the teacher. Due to the merit they accrued from the sādhana (practice) they did in previous births, they are born highly intelligent in this life. Their own intelligence and wisdom become their Guru. They live in the knowledge of the Self, and constant contemplation that "I am brahman and the world I see is an appearance of brahman." The second type of seekers are those who have acquired some knowledge and are committed to the teaching. They do not depend as much on a Guru. They consider the scripture itself a teacher. Based on their faith in the scripture, they study and contemplate on the teaching and attain Self-Knowledge. The third type of seekers do not have such a sharp intelligence. They are not capable of reading the scripture and grasping the truth on their own. They need the help of a teacher to read and understand the scripture. With the help of a teacher they quickly attain Self-Knowledge. The fourth type of seekers are dull and incapable of grasping anything on their own. They certainly need a teacher. By serving a teacher and listening to the teaching constantly, their minds get gradually purified, and in time, will turn towards Self-Knowledge.

In this manner, the first two types of seekers may not require a teacher, but the last two types certainly need one. Even though it might appear as though the first type of seekers, the highly qualified ones, do not require a teacher in this life time, they certainly must have had served an eminent teacher in their previous lives because their highly refined minds are capable of quickly grasping the highest knowledge in this current lifetime. There is no effect without a cause. Therefore, we should not carelessly dismiss the need for a teacher. If we try to learn on our own without the guidance of a teacher, we might end up on a wrong path in our confusion.

We need not be surprised that a Guru is necessary. A Guru is one who has attained complete Knowledge of the Self, the same complete knowledge that the scripture offers. This knowledge is none other than Advaita, the knowledge of the Non-Dual Self. Such knowledge can be acquired only through an accomplished Advaita teacher and teaching, and not through a dualistic teacher and teaching. We need not worry that our intelligence will be compromised if we seek the help of an accomplished teacher. Since the teaching is on the essence of Advaita, the seeker can be rest assured that he or she will only benefit from the teaching. Since the teacher has direct experience of the Self, he is śiva-svarūpa, Supreme Consciousness Itself.

19. mahāvidyā

She who is the seat of exalted knowledge, the knowledge of the Self.

What is that knowledge that an accomplished Guru provides? It is *mahāvidyā*. That which provides knowledge of something is vidyā. There are countless types of vidyā-s in the world. Whatever type of vidyā it may be, whether of the world, tantra, mantra, or yoga, they are all dualistic in nature. Every one of them focuses on a specific knowledge that is different from the subject who is seeking the knowledge. They all invariably involve the triad - the knower, the object to be known, and knowledge. Hence, these worldly knowledges only perpetuate differences, and not dissolve the differences in the Absolute truth.

There is only one type of Knowledge that can offer the Absolute truth. It is the knowledge of Advaita. It dismisses the triad as unreal and establishes the Self as real. Whatever is perceived, it is an appearance only. It is the Self, Pure Consciousness itself that appears as everything. Due to ignorance, we perceive names and forms as real. The wise see everything as śiva, Pure Consciousness. Hence ignorance and knowledge are all based on one's viewpoint. If one were to ask, "where does this ignorance come from?," that very question would be arising from ignorance. Therefore, there is no point in wasting our effort asking such questions. Instead, we must stand firm in our conviction that Self alone IS. This is the highest knowledge that Advaita teaches.

Since Advaita answers all questions, it is the most exalted Knowledge. Since this exalted knowledge is the very nature of the Goddess, She is called *mahāvidyā*. She is also known as *brahmavidyā* (Knowledge of the Supreme Consciousness), *tatvavidyā* (Knowledge of the essence of who we are), etc. Since this non-dual knowledge is taught by the teacher and received by the disciple, this teacher-disciple tradition is the primary means for attaining Self Knowledge.

20. brahmātmaikya svarūpiṇī; 21. tattvamartha svarūpiṇī

She whose nature is the union of brahman and ātmān.

She who is the meaning of tat (that) and tvam (thou).

These nāma-s describe the nature of the great Knowledge that the Guru teaches. The Knowledge is about the Oneness of the jīvā (individual) and brahman (Supreme Consciousness). Brahman is derived from the word bṛhat, which means big and expansive. It is so expansive that it pervades everything - time, space, and objects. Such an expansive entity can only be Consciousness because Consciousness alone can cognize Its expansion. Consciousness is the cognizing principle. It is the spark of I-Am awareness (sphuraṇa) in every being. That spark of awareness is ātmā. There is no difference between the Supreme Consciousness (brahman) and the individual Consciousness (ātmā). Since it is the "I Am" awareness (ātmā) Itself that cognizes everything, brahman is ātmā.

Similarly, ātmā is brahman. Ātmā is the Consciousness that vibrates as the I-Am awareness in this body. It is neither the body nor the life-force (prāṇa) because they are both inert, and appear as objects to awareness. How can that which I am aware of be me? Therefore, although the feeling of "I" appears to be confined to my body and life-force, my real nature is pure Awareness. As Awareness, I am not confined to my body. Like space, I am formless and all-pervading.

Since brahman and ātmā are both formless and all-pervading, they are not different from each other. Since they are not different, they can be experiences as One (*ekātman*). It is the one Consciousness that appears as ātmā inside the body and as brahman outside the body. Due to this apparent difference, brahman is experienced as though different from me (indirect) and ātmān as me (direct). In reality, brahman and ātmā are the same and experienced directly as One (aparokṣa).

The Upanishads convey this knowledge through declarations called mahāvākya-s. These statements declare the unity of jīvātman and paramātman, the individual self and the Supreme Self. The Upanishadic statements that analyze and explain how such unity is possible are called avāntara vākya-s. While the former convey the essential or primary meaning of the entire sentence, the latter explains the meaning of each word in the sentence. With the help of these avāntara vākya-s the complete meaning of the mahāvākya-s can be understood. For instance, in the mahāvākya, *tat tvam asi*, the word *tat* refers to brahman and the word *tvam* refers to jīvā. The meaning of the two words put together conveys the intent or the essence of the mahāvākya.

The meaning of a mahāvākya can be understood based on its primary meaning (vāchyārtha) or its secondary meaning (lakṣyārtha). For instance, the word tvam may be interpreted in its primary sense as "this jīvā" and *tat* as "that brahman." Interpreted in this manner, the two cannot be united into one because each is perceived as manifesting in different upādhi-s (adjuncts). We think jīvā manifests through the body and brahman through the world. As long as there are two upādhi-s or mediums, jīvā and brahman will always appear separate. They cannot merge into one. Therefore, we must interpret the mahāvākya in the secondary sense. We must apply the principle of jahad-ajahal-lakṣaṇā, where only one of the two entities is considered and the other is ignored in order to arrive at the unity of the two. For instance, if we suddenly see someone from the past and say "He is Devadutta," it means we recognize that person for himself without paying any attention to the differences in time and space from the last time we saw him. Similarly, to grasp the truth that the mahāvākya is pointing to, we must disregard the upādhi, the body-mind organism that we identify with, and instead focus on the I-Am Consciousness that vibrates in the body. Similarly, we must disregard the names and forms that appear in the universe, and focus instead on Consciousness, the common substance that pervades the entire universe.

Since the Immutable Consciousness is the substratum of both jīvā and brahman, jīvā and brahman are One. The upādhi-s of jīvā (body/mind/senses) and of brahman (five elements) appear in Consciousness, are not different from Consciousness, and dissolve in Consciousness. If we enquire deeply into the nature of anything in this manner, we will understand its obvious (in the primary sense) and subtle nature (in the secondary sense). This understanding will spontaneously lead to an intuitive realization of its intrinsic nature. Devī personifies this Knowledge of Oneness. It is through the mahāvākya, *tat tvam asi*, that Devī appears as the Guru and imparts this great Knowledge to the disciple.

22. vimarṣarūpiṇī

She who is in the form of vimarṣa.

A disciple must reflect deeply on the Guru's teaching. Deep enquiry into the nature of a thing is *vimarṣa*. It also means repeated contemplation. The Divine Mother is of the nature of vimarṣa. A question may arise at this point. If Knowledge is the only means of realizing the Self, and no action, such as yoga, worship, rituals, etc. can help, what is the use of vimarṣa? Isn't vimarṣa also action? How can it help?

It is true that Knowledge itself is enough to realize the Self. Knowledge of the Self is the Experience of the Self. However, such experiential Knowledge does not arise suddenly on its own. Some effort is certainly necessary. Vimarṣa is such effort. Deep enquiry and contemplation on the mahāvākya, *tat tvam asi*, is vimarṣa. That is the effort required. Simply hearing the two words *tat* and *tvam* is not enough to understand the deeper significance of the mahāvākya. Several questions and doubts will continue to remain. All questions and doubts can be resolved through manana, contemplation on the deeper meaning of the mahāvākya.

Going beyond the primary meaning of a word to its essential meaning is manana. The sentence *tat tvam asi* (that thou art) states the correlation or congruence between the two words *tat* (that) and *tvam* (thou). It states that the two are one. Not just the words but their meanings must also correlate. How is this possible? It is hard for us to visualize the union of jīvā with brahman because the body-mind adjuncts obstruct our vision. Similarly, we cannot visualize the union of brahman with jīvā because the adjuncts of brahman (earth, water, space. etc.) obstruct our vision. To understand the essential meaning of the statement, *tat tvam asi*, we must disregard the adjuncts and simply contemplate on jīvā as brahman. We will then be able to transcend the limitations of the jīvā, and realize the Infinite brahman. However, this is only one aspect of the correlation between the two. Even if the jīvā realizes the infinite nature of Self, it would only be an indirect or mediated experience (parokṣa). Brahman will still appear as separate from him. To get rid of this feeling of separateness, the jīvā must now contemplate on brahman as his own intrinsic Self. He will then experience brahman directly (aparokṣa). When he contemplates in this manner from all angles that he is brahman and brahman is he, the jīvā will transcend duality and experience his Self as the Supreme Self.

Hence, an earnest seeker must practice not only śravaṇa (listening), but also manana (contemplation) continuously. After he has done enough manana, cleared all his doubts and has a crystal clear understanding of the teaching, he must practice nididhyāsana. He must meditate on the teaching until it becomes an experiential realization. This is necessary for the seeker to stabilize his Knowledge and abide firmly in the Self. Without such relentless meditation, Knowledge of the Self will appear and disappear like a flash of lightening. Instead of abiding as ātmā, the seeker will find himself once again in duality, suffering the pains and pleasures of anātmā. To ensure he does not relapse once again into duality, the seeker must have one-pointed focus on the common substance (Consciousness) that pervades all particulars and not on the particulars. This process is called nididhyāsana.

When śravaṇa, manana, and nididhyāsana are practiced together, it is vimarṣa. It is through vimarṣa that we find the Self shining everywhere in all Its splendor. This practice is like pounding the paddy. The paddy is pounded until the rice separates from the chaff. Śravaṇa is like pounding the paddy ten times. Manana is like pounding the paddy fifty times. Nididhyāsana is like pounding the paddy a hundred times or until the rice separates from the chaff and becomes visible. This practice of śravaṇa, manana, and nididhyāsana is vimarṣa. It must continue until the seeker and the act of seeking dissolve into the Self, and the Self alone remains.

23. parāpara; 24. prasiddhā

She who is both parā and apara.
She who is celebrated.

These nāma-s reveal the nature of the Goddess, the Supreme Self, that one attains as a result of vimarṣa. She is parāpara, the one who is both superior and inferior. That which is un-manifested and inaccessible to the mind and senses (Consciousness) is parā and that which is manifested and accessible to the mind and senses (world) is apara. Devī permeates both parā and apara. We can experience Her by perceiving parā as apara, Consciousness as the manifested world, and apara as parā, the world as an appearance of Consciousness.

As we discussed earlier, śakti appears as though remote and not in our direct experience. When śakti manifests, It appears as the world. The names and forms we see in the world are permeated by citsakti, Consciousness. Therefore, when we see names and forms, we must cognize the underlying Consciousness that pervades them. When we do so, forms will appear as the formless and the formless will appear as forms. There will be no difference between the two. Everything will appear as one undivided whole. These mantras are pointing to that One Universal Consciousness, which is the very nature of Devī who is both form and formless.

A seeker must be capable of such deep enquiry and contemplation. The phenomenal world is always visible. We not only see forms, such as buildings, etc., we also see formless entities, such as space. Because space is formless, it pervades every object internally as well as externally. Isn't it strange that we see the formless space the same way as we see forms? Both are objects to our awareness and we see them both (object and surrounding space) in the same instance. Yet we cannot integrate the two. We see them as separate entities, one as a solid object and the other as empty space. If we can train our minds to perceive names and forms as solidified space, we will be able to cognize parā, the supreme un-manifested formless Consciousness that pervades every object. A refined mind is capable of such a vision.

Earnest seekers will find this practice extremely useful. As they mature in the practice, names and forms will lose their specificity, and everything will appear as space. When forms lose their specificity, there will be no difference between apara and parā, the manifest and the un-manifest. As described in Katha Upanishad (2-10), everything will appear as one: "What indeed is here, the same is there; what is there, the same is here; from death to death he goes; who sees here as if different."

When the division between parā and apara vanishes, Self is perceived as everything and everything as the Self. Devī will appear in Her essential form as Pure Consciousness. We will see Her effortlessly everywhere. Effort is necessary only if She is visible sometimes and not at other times. As the Self, She is ever present. No effort is necessary to grasp one's own Self. Therefore, Devī is *parāpara prasiddhā* for the one who realizes Her true nature.

25. bhāvanāgamyā; 26. dhyānagamyā

She who can be attained through imagination.
She who is to be attained through meditation.

The meditation suggested in the previous verse is for mature seekers with sharp and highly refined intellects. Others may find it difficult to grasp. Even if they are able to grasp it, they may not be able to retain or abide in it. The subtler a thing is, the harder it is to grasp it, even if it is present directly in front of us. The eyes may see it, but the mind may not register it. Imagination is necessary in such situations. The formless all-pervading nature of Devī can be grasped only through imagination and visualization. That is why Devī is called bhāvanā. The more one visualizes and meditates on Her, the more Her shining presence is revealed.

What does the word bhāvanā mean? It is a popular term in Ayurveda, often used in the context of amalgamating different types of herbs to make different types of medicines. The process whereby one substance acquires the attributes of another substance is called bhāvanā. Another word for bhāvanā is vāsanā (impression). The term Īśāvāsya means applying the essence of Iśvara on the entire world, so that the world is experienced as Iśvara or Consciousness.

We must apply the same understanding here as well. We must ascribe (bhāvanā) the qualities of ātmā, sat-cit (Existence-Consciousness), to the world and perceive the world as ātmā. As we mature in such contemplation, names and forms will fade into the background and *sat-cit* will appear in the foreground. The form of Devī as *sat-cit* will appear everywhere at all times. To make sure she does not appear and disappear like a bolt of lightning, we must meditate on Her continuously without a break. Devī is accessible through relentless meditation. Mediation is one-point concentration. Like the uninterrupted flow of oil, if we meditate on the nature of Devī continuously without a break, She will be established in our minds firmly as *sat-cit*. Everything - the mind that thinks, the words that express, and the body that acts – will be experienced as *sat-cit*.

27. dhyānadhyātṛ dhyēyarūpā

She who shines as meditator, meditation, and object of meditation.

When bhāvanā (visualization) is continuous and steady, it culminates in meditation. Meditation culminates in experiential realization. Since the realization is of our own Self, it is really not meditation, since there is no separate object to be meditated on and no separate subject that is mediating. The triad, meditator-meditation-object of meditation, all dissolve into the Self. A dualistic mind sees multiplicity. Multiplicity gives rise to feelings such as, "I am the meditator, this is the object of my meditation, and I am meditating." When the object of mediation is one's own Self, there is no scope for a meditator or meditation. The triad dissolve into the Self, who is Devī Herself! As separate entities or together as one, the triad are nothing but Pure Consciousness. This means, multiplicity and uniformity, duality and non-duality, are all of the nature of Devī.

28. nirbhēdā; 29. bhēdanāśinī

She who is beyond all sense of differences.
She who removes from her devotees all sense of differences born out of vāsanā-s.

In reality, these are no differences in Devī. She is pure, undifferentiated Consciousness. The differences are imagined by us due to avidyā (ignorance). Since the differences are only imagined, the moment we stop imagining them, the Goddess will reveal Herself. In reality, neither does She conceal or reveal Herself since She is ever present as pure Consciousness. Concealment and revelation are attributes of the mind. Even if the mind fluctuates between them, Devī remains immutable. The rope is a rope even if it appears as a snake, stream of water, or a stick. Similarly, even though we see names and forms instead of Devī, Devī Herself remains undifferentiated.

The moment we understand Her true nature, we will realize She is Pure Undifferentiated Consciousness. Without such understanding, we will not be able to transcend names and forms. Since She is undifferentiated, She is capable of blessing us with an undifferentiated vision. This is the significance of the mantra *bhēdanāśinī*. Differences are imagined by us, but She is undifferentiated. Only what is real can remove the unreal. We must cultivate a homogenous vision that can cognize the unchanging reality which is the substratum of the changing universe. Like the disappearance of the illusory snake when the knowledge of the rope arises, the heterogenous world disappears in a homogenous vision.

30. nirmamā; 31. nirahaṅkārā

She who has no self interest in anything.
She who is without egoism; She who is without the concept of "me" and "mine."

When the world no longer appears differentiated, the notions of "I" and "mine" disappear. Since names and forms dissolve in ātmā, there is nothing remaining to claim as "mine." When there is nothing left to be attached to, there is no scope for a "me," the separate self to arise. When ātmā reigns supreme everywhere, there is no scope for thieves like "I" and "mine" to enter.

Before the rise of Self-Knowledge, the jīva thinks it is a finite self, limited to the body-mind. It perceives an external world and calls it "mine." Now, after attaining the knowledge of the Self, the body-mind and the external world transform into ātmā. There is no separate entity "I" left to be attached to and to claim anything as "mine." Only when there is a cause, there is an effect. When there is no cause, there is no effect. Similarly, when there are no body and world to get attached to, there is no sense of "I" and "mine."

A question arises at this point. Even after everything transforms into the Self (ātmā), won't the seeker consider the Self as "me" and the world as "my śakti?" In that case, is it possible for the notions of "I" and "mine" to be completely annihilated? This is a valid question. When everything is experienced as ātmā, even if the notions of me and mine continue, there is no problem because they are both experienced as Pure Consciousness. The Self is experienced as Pure Consciousness and not as a body-mind organism. Similarly, since the world is also experienced as Consciousness (śakti*)* even though it appears as "mine," there will be no attachment. Śakti is not different from śiva (Self). Hence, when everything is being experienced as Pure Consciousness, if śiva and śakti manifest as "I" and "mine," it is only joy. This is the essence of these two nāma-s. The prefix "nir" can be interpreted either as total absence or complete presence.

32. mṛtyumathanī; 33. nirbhavā

She who destroys death.
She who is without origin.

When the limited sense of me and mine are destroyed in the Oneness of the Self, there is no more death to the jīvā. Ego (me) and attachment (mine) are the reason for death. Change is death. Only the finite is subject to change, not the Infinite and Immutable. Once we have transcended the finite body and attained the Supreme Self, whatever we perceived earlier as a separate world will now appear as a manifestation of śakti.

When the notion of "I" and "mine" merge into the formless Consciousness, there is nothing left that can change. When there is no change, there is no death. That is why Devī is called *mṛtyumathanī*, the one who destroys death. As the formless, attribute-less Pure Consciousness, Devī transcends death. As the immortal One, She bestows immortality.

Immortality is the very nature of the Self. When we say there is no death, we also mean there is no life after death. Because we forget our immortal nature, we erroneously assume we will die. If we mediate on Devī who is *mṛtyumathanī* (the destroyer of death) as our very own Self, we will realize that death is non-existent. When there is no death, life flows smoothly with no obstruction. Not life as the physical body, but life as Consciousness. Consciousness is ever present, never absent. When we realize there is no death, we also realize there is no birth. The nāma *nirbhavā* signifies this truth. The word bhava means birth. Birth is at one end of life and death at the other end. When there is no end called death, there can be no beginning called birth. The word *mṛtyumathanī* means no death, and *nirbhavā* means no origin or birth. If we contemplate on these nāma-s of Devī, we will transcend birth and death and attain the immortal Self. This is the essence of these two mantras.

34. śāntā; 35. brāhmī; 36. parāniṣṭhā

She who is tranquil.
She who presides over speech.
She who is the Supreme End, the supreme abidance.

When the fear of birth and death is transcended, there is total peace. Birth and death are the reason for unrest and turmoil in human lives. The moment birth and death are transcended, peace is present effortlessly. Unrest begins with birth, continues till death, and resumes with rebirth. When the cycle of birth and death is broken, there is no cause for unrest. Peace alone prevails. The three factors that cause human suffering – physical ailments, natural calamities, and karmic forces – will lose their power on us. We remain at peace because we are no longer pressured by them. The peace mantra (*śānti śānti śānti*) is chanted thrice to address each of the three factors that cause suffering. Peace being Her very nature, Devī can bestow peace on us.

She is not only peaceful (*śāntā*), She is also *brāhmī*, expansive and all-pervasive. She bestows the state of brāhmī, a state of total peace, to those who worship Her. In Bhagavad Gita, Lord Krishna also refers to the brāhmī sthiti in Chapter 2.72, a state that one hopes to attain at the time of death. However, one need not wait for death to experience brāhmī sthiti. It can be experienced even while alive. Because this state of Being is related to brahman, it is called brāhmī. Since brahman is ever present, brāhmī sthiti is also ever present. It is a state that neither rises nor sets.

Devī is not only *śāntā* and *brāhmī*, She is also *parāniṣṭhā*, the Absolute, the Supreme End beyond which there is nothing. Niṣṭhā means the absolute end or completion. Kaṭhopaniṣad (1-3-11) states: "Beyond the great ātmān is the Un-manifested; beyond the Un-manifested is the Puruṣa (the Cosmic Soul); beyond the Puruṣa, there is nothing. That is the end that is the final goal." Since there is nothing beyond Devī, She is *parāniṣṭhā*, the Absolute, the ultimate state of Consciousness. Our purpose is to attain that Supreme state of Devī.

37. hēyōpādēya varjitā

She who has nothing to reject or accept.

The one who attains that Supreme state (parāniṣṭhā) while still embodied is a jīvanmukta. In order to live, the body, mind, and sense organs are necessary. As long as these adjuncts (upādhi-s) are present, transactions with the empirical world are unavoidable. What is the meaning of liberation then?

Even though a jīvanmukta appears to have a body and appears to transact with the world, he maintains equanimity. He neither desires nor rejects anything. He sees no duality since he transcends duality. In reality, there is neither good nor bad in the world. Everything in essence is *sat-cit*, Existence-Consciousness. To the one who sees everything as Self, Pure Consciousness, there is nothing to reject or desire. How can one reject one's own nature? There is nothing to desire either because there is no other to desire. The most desirable entity, Self, is already in our possession. If It has to be newly acquired, It cannot be the real Self.

There can only be one formless and all-pervasive entity. Space is such an entity. It neither desires nor rejects anything. It is not subject to likes and dislikes. When physical space itself is undifferentiated, we can imagine the undifferentiated nature of Devī, who is citākaṣa, Conscious-space. She is everywhere, in everything, and everything is in Her. There is nothing in the universe that is not Her. She is beyond all dualities - good and bad, desirable and undesirable. But She is *mahāmāyā* and *mahāśakti*, the Great Illusion and the Great Power of Illusion that can manifest duality. Her manifestation is Her expansion (vibhūti). Her manifestation abounds in transactions. She engenders dualities, likes and dislikes, and plays with them. In this state, She is not varjita (not devoid of likes and dislikes). These nāma-s can be interpreted in two ways – that Devī is full of polarities (likes and dislikes) or that She is devoid of all polarities. This is also the state of the jīvanmukta who realizes and abides in Devi as Pure Consciousness.

38. abhyāsātiśaya jñātā

She who is known through the exceedingly strenuous practice called spiritual discipline.

A question is likely to arise at this point. Is it possible to experience jīvanmukti in this very lifetime? Since we are not highly qualified (uttamādhikri) like the Sages Vyāsa, Vasiṣṭha, and Suka, is it possible for us also to attain such perfection?

This nāma is a response to that question. Complete abidance in the Self (niṣṭa) is both easy (sulabha) and difficult (durlabha). We must remember that the thousand names of the Divine Mother include the two names, *sulabha* and *durlabha*. As we advance and mature in our practice, we will attain niṣṭa. Practice (abhyāsa) is constant reflection. Bhagavan Krishna and Sage Patañjali unanimously declare renunciation (vairāgya) and relentless practice (abhyāsa) as prerequisites for attaining niṣṭa. There is nothing that cannot be attained with relentless practice in our worldly and spiritual lives.

Practice is not to be measured in terms of the number of times it is practiced or the length of time it is practiced. Practice must continue until the desired results are attained. That is why Sage Patañjali advised practicing aṣṭāṅga yoga continuously with devotion and discipline. Only with such commitment, a seeker can attain maturity. Unwavering focus and relentless effort will produce the desired results. This is in our experience. The more effort a musician puts into practicing music, the sooner she will master the music. The more experienced a cook is, the sooner she will become a master in cooking. Similarly, when the seeker matures in the practice of viewing the world (not-Self) as an appearance of the Self, the practice will eventually culminate in complete abidance in the Self (ātmā). Anātmā (not-self/world) will lose its specificity and dissolve in the Supreme Self. This is brahmaniṣṭa, the unwavering abidance of the Self as the Self in All.

39. maitryādi vāsanālabhyā

She who is to be attained by love and other good dispositions.

To attain such a lofty goal as total abidance in the Self, a seeker must persevere and stay committed to the practice. Mind is conditioned by many inauspicious impressions (aśubhavāsanā) accumulated over many lifetimes. These impressions obstruct our spiritual progress. As long as our minds are controlled by our tendencies, there is no hope for us. Self-abidance will continue to remain out of reach. Therefore, the first step is to get rid of these negative tendencies. The only way to do so is by cultivating positive tendencies or śubhavāsanā-s. The yoga śāstra advocates cultivating four dispositions or qualities: maitrī (friendship), karuṇā (compassion), mudita (joy), and upekṣā (indifference). This nāma refers to these same qualities.

People are of four types: those who are easy going and happy, those who struggle and are unhappy, those who try to perform meritorious deeds, and those who perform cruel deeds. We interact with these four types of people all our lives. When we interact with them closely, we are likely to acquire their tendencies. To make sure their tendencies don't create new tendencies in us, we must counter the negative tendencies with positive tendencies, such as becoming friends with those who are happy, being compassionate to those who are unhappy, rejoicing with those who perform meritorious deeds, and remaining detached from those who perform cruel deeds. Such positive tendencies will remove negative tendencies like envy, stubbornness, intolerance, and hatred. The negative tendencies (aśubhavāsanā-s) will gradually get replaced by positive tendencies (subhavāsanā-*s)*.

As we cultivate strong śubhavāsanā-s, we must let go of good vāsanā-s as well. Even good vāsanā-s are worldly in nature, since they also comprise the three guṇa-s (rajas, tamas, and ṣatva). Vāsanā-s, good or bad, prevent us from attaining and stabilizing our vision in the formless, attribute-less brahman. Therefore, we must transcend both positive and negative tendencies by cultivating a strong vāsanā for brahman, Pure Consciousness. This may not be possible right away. The mind must first be purified with śubha vāsanā-s, and eventually, through deep contemplation and clear understanding of the nature of the Supreme Self, it must transcend all vāsanā-s. As stated in Chāndogya Upanishad 7-26.2, "...from purity of mind comes constant remembrance of God, and from constant remembrance of God, one becomes free of all bondage - one becomes liberated." Therefore, we need not entertain any doubt. A mature seeker is not plagued by doubts. He can easily go to the next step in his practice, quickly reach the peak, and remain there. Therefore, even though a seeker is required to initially cultivate good tendencies and develop strong brahmavāsanā, he must eventually transcend even that vāsanā. As long as strong tendencies persist, they obstruct progress. Positive tendencies purify the mind, but do not help in realizing the Self. When total abidance in the Self is attained, Devī manifests in the seeker as *vāsanā-alabhyā*, the One who transcends all vāsanā-s.

40. ajñānadhvānta dīpikā

She who is the bright lamp that dispels the darkness of ignorance.

The seeker who continues such relentless practice is sure to attain Devī. As Knowledge arises, ignorance, the opposite of Knowledge, disappears. Ignorance, lack of Self-Knowledge, is like a thick veil of darkness. Although it is nothing, darkness appears as though it is something. It is the same with ignorance. Ignorance appears as this expansive world of names and forms. The vṛtti or Knowledge of brahman is like a bright lamp in the darkness called ignorance. Devī is *chidēka rasarūpiṇī.* Like the juice that pervades the entire sugar cane, Consciousness pervades this entire universe. Consciousness (Devī) is like a lamp in the darkness. She shines brightly. Her effulgence spreads widely in all directions. When the light of Consciousness pervades everything completely, there is no scope for the darkness called ignorance to remain. It disappears completely. Like darkness merging into light, the phenomenal world merges into Consciousness. Since Consciousness is the only Reality, It is the only means for getting rid of the ignorance.

41. jñānajñēya svarūpiṇī; 42. sāmarasya parāyaṇā

She who is both knowledge and the known.
She who is immersed in a state of steady wisdom.

In this manner, when the light of Knowledge in the form of a vṛtti of brahman dispels the darkness that appears as the phenomenal world, the great Goddess appears in Her true nature as both subject and object. Aren't subject (knower) and object (known) mutually exclusive entities? How can Devī appear as both? Knower or Knowledge is defined as illumination. When objects are perceived in the light of Consciousness, they lose their particular-ness (get blurred) and dissolve in Consciousness. Consciousness, when It transacts with the object world, appears as the object world. Hence, when we perceive the phenomenal world as a manifestation of Consciousness and not as a separate entity, our vision becomes homogenous and sees only Consciousness everywhere. The world will appear as Consciousness and Consciousness will appear as the world. This homogenous vision is impartial. It does not distinguish between the knower (subject) and the known (object). Both knower and known will be experienced as the Self in all.

Such a homogenous vision and intuitive knowledge of the Self in All is called sāmarasya. The one who sees the Self in all beings, and all beings in the Self is a samadarśi. This is the truth that all the Upanishads proclaim. The subject and the object are ātmā and anātmā respectively. When the two are seen as One, it is sāmarasya. The two become One only when they dissolve completely in the Supreme Self, which is Pure Consciousness. It is the substratum on which everything appears. Expansion of the Self is the world we perceive. Perception of the world as the Self is Knowledge. Knower (ātmā) and known (anātmā) are relative concepts that are dependent on each other. Since they are relative, they can merge into the Absolute. When the knower and the known merge into Pure Consciousness, ātmā alone IS, without a second. That Knowledge is Devī (sāmarasya pārāyaṇa).

43. svasthā; 44. ēkākinī

She who abides in Herself; She who is free from all afflictions.
She who is the lone one.

Complete abidance in the Self (*svasthā*) is the nature of Devī. As pure Consciousness, She stands alone by Herself. Since She alone IS, She can be found only in Herself. For countless births, we have been asleep in ignorance, unaware of Her presence. Gaudapada in Mandukya kārikā (1-16) writes: "When the jīvā or the individual soul sleeping (i.e., not knowing the Reality) under the influence of beginningless māyā is awakened, it, then, realizes (in itself) non-duality, beginningless and dreamless."

When a question arises as to where is māyā located, the Upanishad answers that māyā is located in Her expansion, the phenomenal world.

Although Devī abides in the phenomenal world, we fail to see Her. We see Her manifestation, the microcosm (body/mind, etc.) and macrocosm (earth/space, etc.), but fail to see Her un-manifested presence. Because we see the transient world only, we think Devi is also transient. We fail to recognize Her as the unchanging reality. Since the mind is always outward-facing, it only sees multiplicity. If the mind turns in-wards and sees the unchanging reality, duality (ignorance) will vanish, just like the darkness in the presence of light. Devī will appear as svasthā, Pure Consciousness, free of all afflictions. Since Pure Consciousness is our own nature, we too will be free of all afflictions (svasthā).

When we attain svasthā, we realize that the Self as Pure Consciousness is ever present and that the Self alone IS. Devī is *ēkākinī*, the lone one. Since She alone IS, there is no scope for anything else to be. Even though She is *ēkākinī*, due to Her power of illusion (māyā), She can appear as many. Her appearance as many is the world we perceive. Nāma-s such as *bahurūpa* and *vividhākārā* also indicate the same. Since it is the undifferentiated śakti only that appears as the world, the world is unreal.

Instead of grasping Devī as the One Consciousness that pervades everything, we see Her fragmented into family and possessions. Obsessed with names and forms, we spend our entire life transacting with names and forms. Although our true nature is undifferentiated Consciousness, we see ourselves differentiated into body and mind. Hence, Devī always appears distant and out of reach.

45. duḥkhahantrī; 46. puruṣārthapradā

She who is the destroyer of sorrow.
She who grants the four-fold objects of human life.

The instant the seeker attains the vision of Oneness, all knots of ignorance will fall apart. Sorrow (duḥkha) is one such knot. The scripture refers to the body-mind organism as a dwelling of sorrow. Nobody is exempted from sorrow, neither the rich nor the poor.

We spend all our life trying to get rid of sorrow. But our efforts are in vain. If we manage to get rid of one misery, another pops up. The only way to completely eradicate sorrow is to cultivate a homogenous vision of the Self in all. Since Devī bestows such a vision and frees the seeker from all misery, She is called *duḥkhahantrī*. Since She is *svasthā*, free from all afflictions, She is the destroyer of all afflictions. Sorrow is an affliction. When one realizes that Self alone IS, one is freed from sorrow and other afflictions.

When one is free of sorrow, one can effortlessly attain puruṣārtha, the four goals of human life. As individuals, we are afflicted with likes and dislikes. We are happy when we get what we desire, and unhappy when we get what we do not desire. We crave happiness and shun misery. Hence, happiness is our ultimate goal. The four things we strive for in life (puruṣārtha) are dharma (virtuousness), artha (wealth), kāma (desires), and mokṣa (liberation). The first three goals are worldly (anātmā) in nature. Hence, they can only bring misery and momentary happiness.

The fourth goal, mokṣa brings lasting happiness. There is not even a trace of worldliness in it. Therefore, mokṣa is the ultimate goal of human life. When mokṣa is attained, the other three goals are also attained. There is no need to strive for them separately. Therefore, Devī is called *puruṣārthapradā*, the One who helps us attain both worldly and spiritual goals.

47. svargāpavargadā; 48. nirvāṇa sukhadāyinī

She who bestows heaven and liberation.
She who confers the bliss of liberation.

Not all scholars agree that mokṣa is the only goal to focus on. According to them, scripture is the source of Knowledge on human goals that transcend the world. Since the scripture expounds on both dharma and mokṣa, they are both important. One cannot ignore dharma (attainment of svarga or heaven) and focus only on mokṣa (liberation or apavarga). Unlike ardha (wealth) and kāma (desire) which are worldly goals, dharma and mokṣa are not worldly goals, so they are both equally important

This is not a proper argument. It is true that the scripture instructs on dharma and dharma is different from ardha (wealth) and kāma (desire). It is also true that dharma, like mokṣa, is not of this world, and Devī bestows both. However, there is a big difference between the two. Even though the results of dharma are other-worldly, they do not produce ever-lasting happiness. The happiness they produce is also temporary. Even if a seeker attains a heavenly abode as a result of the merit she acquired from living a virtuous life on earth, the happiness she experiences in heaven is temporary. Once the accrued merit is exhausted, she will have to once again enter a womb, take birth on earth, and continue to experience the pleasures and pains of saṃsāra. The only medicine for this disease called saṃsāra is the complete extinction of all afflictions. Nirvāṇa is the complete extinction of all afflictions, whether of this world or of the other world. That is why mokṣa (liberation) is also called nirvāṇa, the Great Extinction. The happiness derived from mokṣa is the bliss of nirvāṇa. Since Devī bestows such a bliss, She is called *nirvāṇa sukha dāyini*. A true seeker must, therefore, reject even the pleasures of heaven, and strive to attain mokṣa, the one and only worthy goal of human life.

49. sadyaḥ prasādinī; 50. yajamāna svarūpiṇī

She who bestows Her grace immediately.
She who is in the form of yajamāna, the one who directs sacrificial fires.

Liberation is not a goal to be realized only after death. It is possible to attain it right here and now. The moment Knowledge of the Self arises, liberation is attained. Devī is sadyaḥ prasādinī. She bestows results right away. Unlike dharma puruṣārtha, the results of mokṣa sādhana are immediate. A seeker will have to wait until after death to enjoy the results of the dharmic actions he performs in this current life. A question arises at this point. Karma (ritual) is action, and actions produces immediate results. On what basis can we say that the results of the dharmic actions we perform in this current life will come to fruit after death? What is the proof? According to philosophers of mīmāṃsā, Vedic rituals and dharmic actions produce extremely subtle results that are not visible in this life time. According to them, as soon as prārabdha (past karma) is exhausted and the body drops, the jīvā transmigrates to another realm and body, taking with it, in subtle form, the results of its virtuous actions. Hence, the results of dharma puruṣārtha are not immediate.

One the other hand, there is no delay in enjoying the result of mokṣa puruṣārtha. It is immediate. The moment Knowledge rises, mokṣa is experienced because mokṣa is Self-evident, ever-present Consciousness. There is no need to perform any rituals or actions to attain it. Jñāna (Knowledge) alone is necessary. Knowledge or Consciousness is the very nature of mokṣa. Hence, there is no need to go to heaven or some other place to attain it. The triad - individual, heaven, and the act of going there - are all Knowledge. Knowledge is Experience itself. Therefore, there is no means other than Knowledge to attain liberation. If any effort is required, it is only in removing the ignorance that conceals the Knowledge. The way to do so is by realizing that ignorance (anātmā) is also not different from Knowledge. When the Knowledge of the Self rises, anātmā disappears. When anātmā disappears, the seeker, the object sought, and the effort of seeking disappear. Nothing remains. When nothing remains, the seeker who is engaged in jñāna yajna (sacrifice in the form of Knowledge) experiences everything as the Self. That is the reason why Devī is called *yajamāna svarūpiṇī*. Experiencing Devī and Her entire manifestation as one's own Self is Devī presenting Herself as *yajamāna svarūpiṇī*. External rituals and the materials necessary to perform the rituals are not *yajamāna svarūpiṇī*, since they are based on duality. They involve the individual, the act of performing the ritual, materials to perform the ritual, and a heaven or some other world to enjoy the results in. Since the results of external rituals come to fruit only after the death of the current body, there is no way a seeker can verify if this is true. He will have to believe in the scripture. But mokṣa is not like that. Since everything is perceived as one's own Self, one can experience the Self right here and now. There is no need to wait for another life to enjoy the results of our effort to see the One. There is no need to doubt if this is true. The scripture and the direct experience of great sages provide ample evidence. Since mokṣa puruṣārtha produces lasting peace and happiness, it is the supreme goal of human life. Hence, every sincere seeker must strive for Self-Knowledge and make himself or herself worthy of the ultimate experience of the Self.

51. sarvāntaryāminī; 52. pūrṇā

She who dwells inside all.
She who is always whole, without growth or decay.

Because Devī is *yajamāna svarūpiṇī*, it does not mean that only the yajamāni, the one who performs the jñāna yajña, is entitled to mokṣa. Devī, who is Pure Consciousness, is not limited to any form. She resides in everything, sentient and insentient alike. Brihadaranyaka Upanishad declares, "That which resides in everything, pervades everything, contains everything in itself, controls everything – that is ātmā, the in-dweller (antaryāmi)." Devī is the great power, mahāśakti, that pervades everything. Without Her, nothing can exist or appear to exist. In fact, It is śakti that sustains everything. She keeps the moving and unmoving parts of the micro and macro cosmic worlds in motion and performing their respective functions. Sri Krishna says in Bhagavad Gita (18-61): "The Supreme Lord dwells in the hearts of all living beings, O Arjuna, revolving through māyā all the creatures (as though) mounted on a machine."

Devī's mahāśakti is not like the insentient powers we perceive in the world. It is citsakti, Conscious power. Hence, Devī can transform and manifest as anything at Her will. That is why Vedantins refer to Her as pūrṇa (totality), that which permeates everything, moving and unmoving, inside, outside, and in the middle. Every atom is permeated with Consciousness. When Consciousness pervades everything - inside, outside, and in the middle – there is no place for anything else, moving or unmoving, to exist on its own. Since everything is pervaded by and permeated with Consciousness, Consciousness alone IS, with no other.

Sri Krishna in Bhagavad Gita (10-20) echoes this truth when He says, "O Arjuna, I am seated in the heart of all living entities. I am the beginning, middle, and end of all beings."

The peace invocation mantra in Ishavasya Upanishad also echoes this truth: " That is full. This is full. This fullness has been projected from that fullness. When this fullness merges in that fullness, all that remains is fullness."

Therefore, when we don't see any difference between this and that, and when we see everything as the One Consciousness, our vision is pūrṇa (complete). There is nothing to challenge Its completeness. Therefore, Devī is *sarvāntaryāmini*. She is pūrṇa because She permeates everything as Pure Consciousness and manifests in everything as Pure Existence. She is mahāśakti, the all-pervasive Self in all.

53. śāśvatī; 54. śrī śivā

She who is eternal.
She who is the auspicious and divine śiva.

This state of perfection, pūrṇa, is not really a state because it is not transient. It is present at all times - past, present, and future. That which is Self-evident is ever present. Hence, Devī is called *śāśvatī*, the One that is ever present. Results produced by dharmic deeds, such as the attainment of heaven (*svarga*), are not permanent. Mokṣa is permanent. Mokṣa is not absent now. If we say we attained mokṣa now, it implies that we have newly produced or created mokṣa. If we say, we will attain mokṣa in the future, it implies that it is absent now. If it is absent now and must be acquired in the future, there is no comfort because it may be lost in the future. That which can never be negated and is ever present is śāśvatī.

Śaśvatī would have no meaning if one returns to the world after mokṣa. Therefore, mokṣa is not a state like the other states (awake, dream, and deep sleep) that come and go. It is śāśvatī, eternal.

Because Devī is *śāśvatī*, She is also worshiped as śrī śivā - that which is eternal. That which is born and destroyed is śava (corpse). It is saṃsāra. When we transcend saṃsāra, we attain not just śiva, but śrī śivā. The word śrī denotes śakti/energy and śivā denotes Consciousness. Together they are One. The mantra *śivaśaktyaikya rūpiṇī* is yet another nāma of the divine mother that illustrates the unity or oneness of śiva-śakti, Consciousness-Existence.

If śiva and śakti were not united as One, śiva would be a sava (corpse) without śakti, and śakti would have no existence without śiva. Śiva is jñāna śakti (omniscience), and Devī is kriyāśakti (omnipotence). Śrī is the power of execution (kriyāśakti). Śiva is the Knowledge/Intelligence (jñāna śakti). There is no difference between power (śakti) and the one who wields the power (śiva). This is the basic principle. Therefore, śiva and śakti are One. This Oneness of śiva and śakti has been graphically depicted as ardhanārīśvara in the Siva Purāṇa and other mythologies. We must remember that Consciousness and Its creative power (manifestation) are not two separate entities. Together, they are One. It is this realization that frees us from samsara.

Summary

We have now completed a study of the divine names of the Goddess that describe Her ascent. Starting with the nāma, *avyāja karuṇāmūrti* and ending with the nāma *śiva*, the 54 nāma-s describe the ascent of Devī. As we discussed earlier, in reality, Devī neither descends or ascends. It is the jīvā that descends into saṃsāra and ascends to śiva. As long as we are ignorant of our real nature and are controlled by our tendencies, we will find ourselves caught up in the cycle of life and death (saṃsāra). This is our descent. When we attain the knowledge of the Self through continuous contemplation on the Self, we will transcend saṃsāra and attain śiva. This is our ascent. The descent and ascent are only metaphorically ascribed to Devī. Devī is described as vidyā'vidyā svarūpiṇī (of the nature of knowledge and ignorance). It is due to Her avidyā nature that we descend into saṃsāra, and it is due to Her vidyā nature that we ascend to liberation. Since bondage (avidyā) and liberation (vidyā) are two aspects of the one Supreme Power, regardless of where we are, in bondage or in liberation, we are always abiding in Her, since nothing is outside of Her. When we realize this truth, there is no more descent or ascent. We will experience Self as Devī, Pure Consciousness, which is the very nature of our Self (ātmā).

Conclusion

We have selected a subset of 108 names from the 1000 divine names of the Goddess (*Lalitā sahasranāma*), divided them into two parts, and studied them in great detail. The 108 names we discussed in this book are organized in the spirit of the mantra *rahoyāga* (the secret ritual). Since our focus is on mokṣa, we selected nāma-s associated with jñāna (knowledge) and mokṣa (liberation) only and ignored the rest that are associated with yogic and tantric practices.

The 1000 names (*Lalitā sahasranāma*) of the Goddess are also referred to as the secret names of the Goddess (rahasya nāma-s). It is said that the Sage Hayagriva himself had narrated these nāma-s to Sage Agastya. Sage Hayagriva is the Guru and Sage Agastya is his disciple. The word "haya" means Knowledge. Sage Hayagriva is an accomplished teacher, and Sage Agastya is a highly qualified disciple whose mind is sharp as a razor and still as a mountain.

Devi is the Guru. That is why She is praised as *gurumūrti* and *gurumaṇḍala rūpiṇī*. It is stated in Brahmapurāṇa that Sage HayagrIva received the *sahasranāma* (1000 names) from Devī Herself. Sage HayagrIva, who was initiated into the *sahasranāma*, is no other than Lord Ganesha.

Who is Ganesha? How did his birth take place? One of the names of the Divine Mother answers this question: *kāmēśvara mukhālōka kalpita śrī gaṇēśvarā* - He who has manifested out of the union of śiva and śakti is gaṇēśvarā. According to the purāṇas, the karma of the jīva manifests as the desire to create in puruṣa and prakṛti (śiva and śakti). Jīvā-s are created in this manner. Ganesh represents the jīvā. The collection of gross and subtle elements that the jīva is made up of is, gaṇa. The body-mind-vital force is one such collection. Jīvā, the individual Consciousness, is the owner (pati) of this collection (gaṇa). Hence, Gaṇapati is the jīvā himself.

It is this ownership and identification with the gaṇa, body-mind-lifeforce, that is bondage. It forces the jīva to do karma and suffer the consequences of its actions. The feeling of doer-ship and enjoyer-ship are engendered by the mind and prāṇa. The jīvā inherited them from his parents. Jñāna śakti is his father and kriyāśakti is his mother. These two śakti-*s,* in the form of the mind and lifeforce, entered their offspring, Ganesha. However, unlike the parents in whom these powers are fully manifested, the powers are limited in their offspring. Hence, as jīvā-s, we forget the abundance that is our infinite nature, and remain satisfied with our gaṇa, the finite body-mind.

This gaṇa is the saṃsāra for the jīvā. Accordingly, Ganesha gets a huge body with ears, trunk, eyes, and tooth, and a mouse for a vehicle. What does this all mean? Mouse symbolizes a wavering mind. The elephant head symbolizes ego, the sense of doer-ship. Whatever it perceives with its wavering mind, the jīvā consumes it thinking it is a pleasure. That is why his body and ears are huge. His eyes are small. What does that mean? It means that the jīvā hears the teaching about the Self, but lacks the ability to grasp it. Unable to find the joy that transcends all duality, he gets engrossed in the pleasures of the dualistic world. This is the significance of the single tooth/tusk of Gaṇapati. Who are the companions of Gaṇapati? Ghosts and goblins! These are his gross and subtle tendencies (vāsanā-s). Forever trapped and struggling with his tendencies, the jīvā forgets the abundant wealth that he has inherited from his parents. Whatever little wealth he claims, he distributes it between the gaṇa-s, and remains trapped in saṃsāra. This imprisonment in saṃsāra is the tirodhāna power of the Goddess.

If we can win Her grace (anugraha*)* and get out of the grasp of Her tirodhāna power, we will be able to transcend the state of gaṇeśvara and attain the state of *mahāgaṇeśvara*. The jīva who is free of *bhūta gaṇa*, tendencies or vāsanā-s, is *mahāgaṇeśvara.* As long as we are caught up in the obstructive wheel of saṃsāra, Devī's anugraha will remain unattainable. Therefore, we must break this cycle of saṃsāra. How can we do so? We can do so if we can see Consciousness (prakāśa) in every manifestation (vimarṣa). Illumination is śiva, and the illumined is sakti. Only when there is vimarṣa, Consciousness shines. If there is no vimarṣa, Consciousness remain dulls and hidden. It will also appear as something else. That is saṃsāra. It is due to saṃsāra that the jīvā is reduced to *gaṇeśvara.* Once he is awakened, either due to the merit accumulated in past lives or due to the teaching received from a Guru, the jīvā will be able to recognize his true nature (Self) as Consciousness. When his abidance in the Self is unwavering, vimarṣa will break the cycle of saṃsāra and culminate in the state of mahāgaṇeśvara. By the grace of the Divine Mother, the seeker will attain śiva and experience Self as pure Consciousness. This is the meaning of the nāma - *mahāgaṇēśa nirbhinna vighnayantra praharṣitā*

These two nāma-*s* represent the two states of human consciousness. *Kāmēśvara mukhālōka* indicates the state of bondage. *Mahāgaṇēśa nirbhinna* indicates the state of liberation. As discussed earlier, the syllables *ka* and *ra* in the mantra *kāmēśvara* indicate his descent into saṃsāra, and the syllables *tha* and *ra* in the mantra *praharṣitā* indicate his ascent to freedom. Bondage is due to ignorance, and freedom is due to Knowledge. Freedom from bondage is the great accomplishment of mahāgaṇēśa. A discriminating intellect (buddhi) is essential for attaining mokṣa (siddhi). When the intellect is absorbed in the contemplation of śiva, it is *mahābuddhi,* and when it is totally identified with śiva, it is *mahāsiddhi.* The śiva purāṇa describes this poetically as *ganesha* having two wives, namely *buddhi* and *siddhi.*

How can we attain *mahābuddhi* and *mahāsiddhi*? It is through vimarṣa. Constant vimarṣa or discrimination is the only means of attaining *mahābuddhi* and *mahāsiddhi.* That which discriminates is thought (nāma). That which is discriminated is form (rūpa). These are śabda (sound) and ardha (meaning), śakti and śiva respectively. Śakti is the sound or word and śiva is the meaning associated with the sound. Śakti in the form of sound (śabda) or word discriminates (vimarṣa), and śiva as the meaning (ardha) of the sound shines (prakasa). From the gross to the subtlest, śabda labels and differentiates everything (as name and form). As each śabda (sound) merges into ardha (meaning), it gives way to another śabda and ardha. For instance, the word prithvi means earth, the word earth implies water, water implies heat, heat implies air, and air implies space.

This process of vimarṣa does not end with space. Space is inert. It is not self-aware. Hence, the word space implies a sentient entity that is aware of its existence. That entity is Consciousness Itself. It is Self-evident. It does not depend on anything for its existence. It is the source of everything - earth, water, fire, air, space. Therefore, Consciousness is the highest truth. The śabda that points to the highest truth is the highest śabda. It is a buddhi vṛtti, a thought-modification that takes the form of the expansive, formless, unmoving space. Such an expansive śabda is referred to as parāvāk, the great sound. Since both sound and meaning are formless and expansive, in this state, prakāśa and vimarṣa become one. This means śiva and śakti, hidden in the sound and its meaning, are one.

If we continue to contemplate with a discriminating intellect in this manner, we will realize the nature of the Supreme Self. We will transform from the state of gaṇēśa to mahāgaṇēśa. As Sri Krishna says in Bhagavad Gita, only one in a million have such a good fortune. Such an enlightened one will liberate himself as well as others. Seekers like us must take refuge in such enlightened beings, surrender to them, and follow their teaching.

What is the nature of that mahāgaṇēśa who appears in the form of a satguru? The following verse describes the universal characteristics of such a teacher.

shuklambhara-dharam vishnum shashi varnam chatur bhujam
prasanna vadanam dhyaayet sarva vighnopashaanthaye

śukla ambara does not simply mean white garment as it is usually translated. It means Pure Knowledge devoid of all impurities. *Mahāgaṇēśa* is the satguru that abides in the Knowledge of the Self. *Viṣṇum* means that which is expansive. Instead of being limited to a body, his Self expands and permeates everything, He is *sasi varna. Sasi* means moon. Moon represents the mind. While abiding in that non-dual state of Supreme Consciousness that transcends the mind, a satguru occasionally descends to the mind-level to teach Self-Knowledge to aspirants. *Catur bhujam,* the four shoulders, symbolize dharma (virtuousness), jñāna (knowledge), vairāgya (dispassion), and aishvarya (splendor). He who enjoys or experiences these four attributes is *catur bhujam*. Similarly *prasanna vadanam*, is the one who can share the bliss of the Self that he has experienced with others. The Guru who has all these attributes is mahāgaṇēśa. We must seek refuge at the feet of such a Guru and meditate on the teaching (sadā dyāyet) to be free of saṃsāra. Saṃsāra can be mitigated only through brahmajñāna, the knowledge of the Absolute. Every sincere seeker must strive for such knowledge and serve the Guru with one-pointed focus. This is the purport of the verse.

Human life is a great yajña (fire sacrifice). The fire-pit is the ever shining ātmā (Self as Pure Consciousness). The offerings made into the fire are virtuous and un-virtuous actions (dharma and adharma) called saṃsāra. The source of saṃsāra is avidyā (nescience). Avidyā must be scooped up into the ladle called no-mind (unmaṇi) with the two hands called prakāśa and vimarṣa and offered into the fire-pit called ātmā continuously. When we do so, everything that is perceived as anātmā will burn into ashes, and ātmā alone will shine in all Its splendor. This is the reward of meditating on the Divine Names.

Hymn to Lord Dakṣiṇāmūrti

(Commentary on Sri Adi Shankara's Dakṣiṇāmūrti Stotram)

Author's Preface

The advent of Sri Shankaracharya is a great boon to humankind. As a world teacher, Shankara declared unequivocally, without any compromise, that the Knowledge of the Self is the main goal of human life. He taught and wrote extensively to establish this truth. People of his times had the good fortune of hearing his teaching directly from him. Centuries later, we too have the good fortune of reading his elaborate commentaries and teachings. So lucid are his teachings and so profound are our insights when we contemplate on his writings that, even today, we feel his presence. That is why, when people ask me who is my Guru, I reply without any hesitation that Shankara Bhagavadpada is my Guru.

Shankara has left behind a huge collection of works. His works can be grouped into three categories, each group targeting a particular type of seeker based on his or her ability to grasp the teaching. His elaborate commentaries on the Prasthānatraya (Upanishads, Brahma Sutras, and Bhagavad Gita) target the most advanced of seekers; his treatises, such as the Upadeśa Sahasri, target the average seeker, and the various hymns he wrote, such as the Dakṣiṇāmūrti Stotra, target the beginner. Every one of these works is a precious gem. Big or small, whether it is a commentary or a hymn, his writings spread the same divine light of Pure Non-Dual Consciousness everywhere. Whichever text we pick, we will find in it, the complete teaching of Advaita. Our responsibility is to extract that knowledge, understand it thoroughly, and experience it for ourselves.

This is the reason why I wrote Prasthānatraya, Jagadguru Mahopadesam, and Sādaka Gita in Telugu. I researched Shankara's works extensively, extracted the essence of his Advaita teaching, and presented it in the form of these books to Advaita seekers in Telugu. I also wrote a commentary on Shankara's Nirvāṇa Daśaka to reveal the profound insights hidden in them. I had a similar desire to write a commentary on the Dakṣiṇāmūrti Stotra. A crown jewel amongst all of Shankara's hymns, the hymn to Dakṣiṇāmūrti is in a class by itself. Although it is a short hymn of ten verses only, it is densely packed with the same profound wisdom that Shankara packed into his extensive commentaries on the Prasthānatraya. If we can read and absorb the wisdom contained in these short verses, we would not have to read anything else. Perhaps, that is why Shankara's prominent disciple, Sri Sureshwarācārya, wrote an elaborate commentary (vartikā) on this hymn, called *Mānasollāsam*, which translates into "that which rejoices the mind."

Dakṣiṇāmūrti Stotra has won great fame and popularity. Based on the title, it may appear as though this hymn is meant for dualists and ritualists, not non-dual seekers whose practice, as advocated by Shankara himself, is only Self-enquiry. In this hymn, Shankara says, "I bow to the Guru, the Lord Dakṣiṇāmūrti." Who is this Guru? Is He different from the Lord? Are the Lord and the Guru in essence One? For a casual reader, the hymn might read like a devotional (bhakti) or ritualistic (upāsanā) rendering. Based on this popular notion, many scholars have written corresponding commentaries. Even Sureshwarācārya, Shankara's foremost disciple, seems to sway somewhat in favor of a ritualistic interpretation in his commentary because, at the end of his work (*Mānasollāsam*), he describes in detail the form of Lord Dakṣiṇāmūrti, the mantra for invoking Him, and the process for worshiping Him. However, Sureshwarācārya may have done so merely to draw the attention of devotional types who worship the formless with form and attributes.

Lord Dakṣiṇāmūrti is not a deity like Shiva or Vishnu who are worshipped with forms and attributes. I personally strongly believe that Shankara's intention is to propagate Self-Knowledge, and not ritualist worship through this hymn. Only then will this hymn be consistent with the rest of his works, which are essentially Advaita in purport. Duality is a common experience. Shankara need not propagate it specifically through this work. Ritualists have already done so quite extensively. There is no need for Shankara to duplicate their work. Shankara's core message is about the ultimate goal of human life, a topic that few, if any, touched on. Hence, his entire teaching is focused on the essence of Advaita and nothing else. This becomes quite obvious to anyone who studies Shankara's works attentively.

The hymn to Dakṣiṇāmūrti must be interpreted in the spirit of Advaita, and not upāsanā (ritualistic worship). When we say we bow to Lord Dakṣiṇāmūrti, it means we bow to the Guru, the Great Teacher, who is Pure Consciousness Itself. Since the essential nature of the disciple is also Pure Consciousness, the Guru is the disciple as well! Therefore, the one who bows and the one who receives the bow are not different. They appear outwardly as two separate entities, but as Consciousness, they are one and the same. This expansive feeling of Oneness, this expereince that I Am everything, is called sarvātmabhāva. Shankara reveals this truth through this hymn. He does so explicitly in the last verse of the hymn when he says, *"sarvātma iti sphuṭīkṛtamidam."*

Lord Dakṣiṇāmūrti represents the union of the masculine and the feminine aspects of creation and is graphically depicted as half masculine and half feminine. He represents the One Consciousness that appears as though split into two, the manifest and the un-manifest.

The dakṣiṇa or the right side of the Lord symbolizes jñāna or Self-Knowledge. The vāma or the left side of the Lord symbolizes His creative power. The word vāma means "vomit." Action or creation is the "vomit" of jñāna. It is the not-self that manifests out of the Supreme Self. Without action (power or śakti), there can be no creation. Without Knowledge or Consciousness, there can be no action. When jñāna alone Is in Its intrinsic nature, Its creative power or śakti lies dormant in Its womb. Therefore, in every reference to Consciousness, there is an implied reference to Its inherent creative power. Hence, Lord Dakṣiṇāmūrti symbolizes the Un-manifested Pure Consciousness.

Guru is an embodiment of Pure Knowledge or Consciousness. Lord Dakṣiṇāmūrti is such a Guru. Having received the teaching from Him and having contemplated on it, His disciples also become teachers and teach other earnest seekers. Hence, a Guru is both a teacher as well as a disciple. Since it is Consciousness Itself that reveals Its true nature, It is the Guru. Since the disciple receives that Knowledge and experiences the Self directly, that Consciousness is the disciple as well. When we contemplate in this manner on the teacher-disciple tradition, we realize that the three (teacher, teaching, and the taught) are in essence One. Lord Dakṣiṇāmūrti symbolizes this Oneness.

This is the significance of the hymn to Lord Dakṣiṇāmūrti. The hymn starts with Dakṣiṇāmūrti (Supreme Self), and ends with Dakṣiṇāmūrti. This is the purport of Shankara's hymn. I named my commentary *Dakṣiṇāmūrti Pradakṣiṇa* to convey this message. *Dakṣiṇāmūrti Pradakṣiṇa* translates into "Circumambulating the Lord Dakṣiṇāmūrti."

A few years ago, I wrote a commentary on this hymn in Sanskrit, and later rewrote it in Telugu and revised it a couple of times to enhance the flow. The transitions from one verse to the next are much smoother in this latest version, and adhere more closely to Shankara's style of writing. I explained the entire verse and embedded the meanings of some terms and phrases within the explanation. This made it possible not only to present a comprehensive explanation of the verse, but also to stay focused on the main point under discussion without deviation. If, occasionally, it appears as though I deviated from the main point, it is only because I was trying to elaborate on some important concepts that Shankara may have merely hinted at in his original verse. As long as the commentary runs in Shankara's style and voice, I believe there will be no room for confusion.

If you ask me why I chose to write a commentary on yet another work of Shankara, I can only answer in Shankara's own words. When Shankara was asked why he wrote such elaborate commentaries on the Upanishads, Brahma Sutras, and so on. Shankar replied that his hope was that his disciples will be able to grasp at least a few hundreds, out of the thousands of verses he had written, and get a crystal clear understanding of the goal of human life.

This is my desire as well – that earnest seekers grasp the profound Advaitic truths buried in these ten profound verses and experience the Truth directly for themselves. Like a moth transforming into a butterfly, if their separate selves (jīvātman) expand to become One with the Supreme Self (paramātman), I will consider my desire fulfilled.

– Yellamraju Srinivasa Rao

– Vijayawada, AP, India

Sep 2014

Sri Dakṣiṇāmūrti Stotram

मौनव्याख्या प्रकटित परब्रह्मतत्त्वं युवानं
वर्षिष्ठांते वसद् ऋषिगणैः आवृतं ब्रह्मनिष्ठैः ।
आचार्येन्द्रं करकलित चिन्मुद्रमानंदमूर्तिं
स्वात्मारामं मुदितवदनं दक्षिणामूर्तिमीडे ॥१॥

विश्वं दर्पणदृश्यमाननगरीतुल्यं निजान्तर्गतं
पश्यन्नात्मनि मायया बहिरिवोद्‌तं यथा निद्रया ।
यः साक्षात्कुरुते प्रबोधसमये स्वात्मानमेवाद्वयं
तस्मै श्रीगुरुमूर्तये नम इदं श्रीदक्षिणामूर्तये ॥1॥

बीजस्याऽन्तरिवाङ्‌रो जगदिदं प्राङ्ङ्निर्विकल्पं पुनः
मायाकल्पितदेशकालकलना वैचित्र्यचित्रीकृतम् ।
मायावीव विजृम्भयत्यपि महायोगीव यः स्वेच्छया
तस्मै श्रीगुरुमूर्तये नम इदं श्रीदक्षिणामूर्तये ॥2॥

यस्यैव स्फुरणं सदात्मकमसत्कल्पार्थकं भासते
साक्षात्तत्त्वमसीति वेदवचसा यो बोधयत्याश्रितान् ।
यत्साक्षात्करणाद्भवेन्न पुनरावृत्तिर्भवाम्भोनिधौ
तस्मै श्रीगुरुमूर्तये नम इदं श्रीदक्षिणामूर्तये ॥3॥

नानाच्छिद्रघटोदरस्थितमहादीपप्रभा भास्वरं
ज्ञानं यस्य तु चक्षुरादिकरणद्वारा वहिः स्पन्दते ।
जानामीति तमेव भान्तमनुभात्येतत्समस्तं जगत्
तस्मै श्रीगुरुमूर्तये नम इदं श्रीदक्षिणामूर्तये ॥4॥

देहं प्राणमपीन्द्रियाण्यपि चलां बुद्धिं च शून्यं विदुः
स्त्रीबालान्धजडोपमास्त्वहमिति भ्रान्ता भृशं वादिनः ।
मायाशक्तिविलासकल्पितमहाव्यामोहसंहारिणे
तस्मै श्रीगुरुमूर्तये नम इदं श्रीदक्षिणामूर्तये ॥5॥

राहुग्रस्तदिवाकरेन्दसदृशो मायासमाच्छादनात्
सन्मात्रः करणोपसंहरणतो योऽभूत्सुषुप्तः पुमान् ।
प्रागस्वाप्समिति प्रबोधसमये यः प्रत्यभिज्ञायते
तस्मै श्रीगुरुमूर्तये नम इदं श्रीदक्षिणामूर्तये ॥6॥

बाल्यादिष्वपि जाग्रदादिषु तथा सर्वास्ववस्थास्वपि
व्यावृत्तास्वनुवर्तमानमहमित्यन्तः स्फुरन्तं सदा ।
स्वात्मानं प्रकटीकरोति भजतां यो मुद्रयाभद्रया
तस्मै श्रीगुरुमूर्तये नम इदं श्रीदक्षिणामूर्तये ॥7॥

विश्वं पश्यति कार्यकारणतया स्वस्वामिसम्बन्धतः
शिष्याचार्यतया तथैव पितृपुत्राद्यात्मना भेदतः ।
स्वप्ने जाग्रति वा य एष पुरुषो मायापरिभ्रामितः
तस्मै श्रीगुरुमूर्तये नम इदं श्रीदक्षिणामूर्तये ॥8॥

भूरम्भांस्यनलोऽनिलोऽम्बरमहर्नाथो हिमांशु पुमान्
इत्याभाति चराचरात्मकमिदं यस्यैव मूर्त्यष्टकम्
नान्यत् किञ्चन विद्यते विमृशतां यस्मात्परस्माद्विभोः
तस्मै श्रीगुरुमूर्तये नम इदं श्रीदक्षिणामूर्तये ॥9॥

सर्वात्मत्वमिति स्फुटीकृतमिदं यस्मादमुष्मिन् स्तवे
तेनास्य श्रवणात्तदर्थमननाद्ध्यानाच्च संकीर्तनात् ।
सर्वात्मत्वमहाविभूतिसहितं स्यादीश्वरत्वं स्वतः
सिद्ध्येत्तत्पुनरष्टधा परिणतं चैश्वर्यमव्याहतम् ॥10॥

Meditation

ōṃ maunavyākhyā prakaṭita parabrahmatattvaṃ yuvānaṃ
varṣiṣṭhāntē vasadṛṣigaṇairāvṛtaṃ brahmaniṣṭhaiḥ I
āchāryēndraṃ karakalita cinmudramānandamūrtiṃ
svātmārāmaṃ muditavadanaṃ dakṣiṇāmūrtimīḍē II 1 II

The Lord Dakṣiṇāmūrti sits under the banyan tree facing the south. The teacher of all teachers, He provides the ultimate knowledge of the Self to seekers of the world. With a face resplendent with Divine Consciousness, He revels in the bliss of His own Self, in the Knowledge that He alone Is without a second. Seated around Him are His disciples, the wise sages Vashista, Vāmadeva, and others. The disciples are old, but the teacher is youthful. What can such a young one teach these wise old men, one wonders. With His hand held in cin-mudra, (a gesture where the index finger and the thumb are held together to form a circle, symbolizing the union of the separate self with the Supreme Self), the Lord silently transmits the knowledge of the Supreme Self to His disciples who also sit quietly around Him, absorbed in the Self.

With a burning desire for Knowledge and liberation, I bow in reverence to Lord Dakṣiṇāmūrti, the embodiment of Self-Knowledge.

Verse 1. The World Is a Reflection in Consciousness

viśvaṃ darpaṇa-dṛśyamāna-nagarī tulyaṃ nijāntargataṃ
paśyannātmani māyayā bahirivodbhūtaṃ yathā nidrayā ।
yassākṣātkurute prabhodhasamaye svātmānamēvādvayaṃ
tasmai śrī gurumūrtaye nama idaṃ śrī dakṣiṇāmūrtaye ॥ 1 ॥

This vast universe with its countless objects, moving and unmoving entities, manifests externally as the objects we see and internally as feelings, perceptions, and emotions. In this first verse, Shankara inquiries into the nature of the world (jagat), the nature of the Creator (Iśvara), and the individual (jīvā) who feels helplessly trapped between the world and the Creator.

Shankara focuses on jagat (world) in the very first stanza because jagat is distinctly visible and ever present, while Iśvara and jīvā are not visibly present. From what is present and visible, the invisible and the absent can be inferred. The world that we see and transact with every moment of our life is the source of our suffering. The jīvā cannot be a problem to himself, nor can Iśvara who is not visible. A problem arises only when two entities of different natures confront each other. For instance, the poison in a snake does not harm the snake because the snake and its poison are one. Similarly, an individual is not a threat to himself. A snake, even if it is poisonous, if it is in a distant place, it cannot harm us. Similarly, Iśvara, who is in some distant place and invisible to us, is not a problem. Hence, it is the world that we confront every moment of our lives that is the problem. It is neither too close to us like our self nor too far away like Iśvara.

Once the problem with the world is resolved, the problem with the individual and Iśvara will also resolve automatically. The notion of a separate world gives rise to the notion of a separate individual.

With the disappearance of the notion of a separate world, the notion of a separate individual also disappears. The world is the upādhi, the adjunct, through which Infinite Consciousness manifests as the finite individual (jīvā). If there are no upādhi-s to manifest, Consciousness will remain in Its own intrinsic nature - Formless, Immutable, Infinite, and Complete. There will be no separate individual. It is the perception of a separate world that gives rise to the notion of a separate individual and a Creator (Iśvara). As long as we think we are limited individuals, Iśvara will appear as different from us. When the finite individual Consciousness expands and permeates the entire world, it dissolves in the Infinite Consciousness without a trace. When the separate self disappears, the separate world and Creator will also disappear.

Hence, even though there appear to be three separate entities, jīvā, jagat, and Iśvara, it is only the jagat that is a source of suffering. To realize our full potential as the Infinite Consciousness, we must understand the nature of the world and how it keeps us in bondage. When all traces of worldly attachments and egoic tendencies are eliminated and Self alone IS, the jīvā is no longer in bondage. All effort must therefore be spent in addressing the source of the problem, which is the world. Hence, Shankara starts the very first verse of the hymn with the word viśvaṃ (universe).

Is the world real? Does it really exist? If we insist that that the world really exists, we will only be reinforcing the problem and not solving it. To solve the problem, we must establish that the world is only an appearance and not real. Even if we establish that the world is not real, one may ask, won't we continue to see it? Isn't it ridiculous to deny the existence of the world when we experience it every minute of our lives? Just knowing that the world is unreal will not make any difference to our experience. Isn't experience the greatest proof of the existence of anything?

So we now face a dilemma. If we say that the world does not exist, it would be a lie because we are experiencing it every minute. If we say that the world does exist, we will only be confirming the problem, not solving it. Shankara skillfully resolves this dilemma using the analogy of a mirror. If we put a large mirror in front of a city, the entire city will appear in the mirror. Is the city that appears in the mirror real? Does it really exist? Since the city is clearly visible to us in the mirror, we cannot deny its existence. But did the city actually enter the mirror? Can something so large as a city completely enter a small mirror? The city in the mirror appears only as long as the mirror is present, and disappears the moment the mirror is removed. What we see in the mirror is only a reflection, not the object itself. The object is outside the mirror. It is not dependent on the mirror in any way for its existence. The object can stand on its own, whether or not the mirror is present. Therefore, the object is real, but the reflection is unreal.

Like the reflection in the mirror, the world that we perceive is a reflection in our mirror-like Consciousness. Consciousness is Real but not visible to our senses. The reflection is visible but it is unreal.

An objection may be raised at this point. In the analogy of the mirror, the city outside the mirror is real and its reflection inside the mirror is false. But now we are saying that the mirror-like Consciousness is real, and the world that is reflected in it is unreal. Perhaps the analogy of the mirror is not appropriate to explain the unreality of the world, one may ask. This is a reasonable concern. However, the purpose of an analogy is only to illustrate a few similarities between two entities. It is enough if it serves the specific purpose that it is intended for, and not much more. Shankara is illustrating only one point through the analogy of the mirror – that the original image is real and the reflected image is false. The analogy, however, is not meant to be extended to explain other aspects. To illustrate these other aspects, Shankara uses yet another analogy – the analogy of a dream.

Let us say we saw a wonderful city in our dream last night. Where did the city come from? Where is it located? Was it inside us or outside us? In the dream, the city appeared as though it is outside us, but when we wake up in the morning, we don't see the city outside. Even when we saw the objects as though outside us in the dream, they were not outside. They were inside us. Therefore, even though we saw the city in the dream, it is a false appearance.

Similarly, whatever is present in our Consciousness is real, and whatever appears outside is only its reflection (ābhāsa). Therefore, the world is unreal. We perceive objects only when they appear within the sphere of our Consciousness. If an object is outside our Consciousness or if our Consciousness does not extend to it, it will not be known to us. If a thing is not "known" to Consciousness, the thing has no existence. Knowledge, Awareness, or Consciousness is the proof of the existence of anything. Therefore, although the entire world is present inside our Consciousness, just like the objects in a dream, they appear as though outside us. Dream objects appear outside us when we are asleep. The world appears outside us when we are awake because of the illusory power of māyā or avidyā. Avidyā is ignorance, lack of Self-Knowledge. Ignorance of our real nature (Self) is present in our dream and waking states. When we are asleep and oblivious of our body and mind, a world appears from inside us as a dream. Similarly, in the waking state, we are oblivious of our true nature as Pure Consciousness and identify with our body and mind. This is māyā. It is due to māyā that Consciousness appears as the external world. It is the attachment and involvement with the illusory world that keeps us in bondage.

To free ourselves from this bondage, we must find the source of the problem and remove it. Ignorance is the source of the problem. Knowledge is the solution. Attaining Knowledge is prabodha. The word prabodha has two meanings: Awakening and Intelligence. Both of these meanings are applicable here. When we wake up from a dream and realize that what we saw is a dream, it is prabodha (awakening). In the larger context of our lives, when Knowledge arises, prabodha means Intelligence. When Knowledge of the Self arises, we realize that Self is pure Awareness, and that it has always been present as the "I Am" awareness even before the dawn of Knowledge. This "I Am" awareness that we had prior to Knowledge, however, is not pure non-dual awareness of the Self. In addition to the sense of "me," that awareness also included the sense of the "other," the world with its animate and inanimate objects. This sense of "other" limits the Self and perpetuates wrong notions, such as "I am a limited individual" and "there is a Creator who is superior to me somewhere." It is these wrong notions that are māyā. The moment we realize that this external world is unreal, we will be free of māyā. When we are free of māyā, the world disappears. Instead of multiplicity, we will perceive everything as non-dual Oneness.

What do we gain by such a vision? When the world dissolves into the Self, the world ceases to be a problem. When there are no limiting adjuncts, such as body, mind, and the world, the Self freely expands into the Universal Self. With its expansion, the separate self disappears. Since the Universal Self is Iśvara, the notion of a Creator also disappears. Instead of appearing as three separate entities, jīvā, jagat, and Iśvara dissolve into the Self, which is Pure Undifferentiated Consciousness. This is the experience of the Supreme Self or Universal Self. The Lord Dakṣiṇāmūrti symbolizes the Supreme Self (paramātma). The word dakṣiṇa means Knowledge or Intelligence (jñāna śakti), and the word vāma means, the power to act or create (kriyā-śakti). Intelligence is the very nature of the Supreme Self. Creation is Its expansion (vibhūti). Since the creative power is intrinsic to the Supreme Self, Dakşiṇāmūrti is a complete and perfect union of the jñāna śakti and kriyā śakti. The Supreme Self is the Guru. The disciple who attains the perfection of his Guru is also Dakşiṇāmūrti. Hence, the teacher and the disciple who attain perfection through the teaching are both brahman. Although Shankara says he bows to the three (teacher/teaching/disciple), in essence he bows to the One who is Pure Consciousness.

Verse 2. World Manifests From ātmā Like a Seedling from a Seed

bījasyāntari-vāṅkurō jagadidaṃ prāṅgnirvikalpaṃ punaḥ
māyākalpita dēśakālakalanā vaicitryacitrīkṛtam I
māyāvīva vijṛmbhayatyapi mahāyogīva yaḥ svecchayā
tasmai śrīgurumūrtaye nama idaṃ śrī dakṣiṇāmūrtaye II 2 II

Everything is of the nature of the Self, Pure Consciousness. This can be experienced as true only if the world disappears completely. It must cease to exist not only externally, but also internally. On one hand, Shankara says in the previous verse that the world is inside us (*nijāntargataṃ*) and, on the other hand, he says the Self is non-dual (*advayam*). If the world is inside the Self, how can the Self be non-dual? What does the word "inside" really mean? When a thing is inside another thing, how can the thing inside be same as the thing outside? For example, if a book is inside a box, how can the book be the same as the box? Similarly, if the world is inside me, the world cannot become same as me. If there are two entities, it is duality, not non-duality.

Shankara addresses these questions in this second verse with the analogy of a seedling. He says, the world is inside the Self, just like a seedling is inside a seed. Before it manifests externally as a plant, the seedling is inside the seed. Because it is already present inside the seed, it is able to appear outside. Nothing can appear suddenly out of nowhere. If a thing that is visible now was not visible previously, it is only because it was hidden in its source. Because it was present inside, it could manifest outside. This is common experience.

Another question now arises - how can a thing that is inside something be the same as the thing that contains it? The seedling analogy answers this question as well. The seedling came out of the seed. Before it came out, it was hidden inside the seed. What was the nature of the seedling when it was inside the seed? Was it the same as the seed or different from it? If we break open the seed and see, we will find a single undifferentiated substance, which is the seed itself. We don't see any duality inside the seed.

Similarly, there is no duality in Consciousness (prajñā). Before its external manifestation, the world with its animate and inanimate objects is present un-manifest and undifferentiated in Consciousness. When we say the world is inside Consciousness, we are not suggesting a dependent relationship between them because Consciousness is a single homogenous substance. If Consciousness is a homogenous substance, how can it contain a world inside it? Due to ignorance, we imagine a world outside our Consciousness. To correct our misapprehension, Shankara first provisionally says that the world is inside us, but, later, to make sure we do not assume that there are two separate entities, he says that the world is inside us as undifferentiated Consciousness.

Just like the undifferentiated seed that manifests externally as a sprout, undifferentiated Consciousness manifests externally as the world. Because of the energy that is intrinsic to it, the seed itself manifests externally as a seedling. This power or energy is formless, hence it is undifferentiated from its source (Consciousness). Power and the one who wields the power are not two separate entities. The seed and its energy are a single entity. It is this energy in the seed that transforms into a seedling. In reality, it is not a transformation. It is only an appearance, an illusion that the seed has transformed into a seedling. Whether it is a sprout, a plant, or a tree, wherever we touch and feel it, we will only touch and feel the attributes of the seed and nothing else. Therefore, it is the seed itself that appears as a sprout, plant, etc. because of its inherent ability to manifest in these forms.

Similarly, ātmā or the Self is undifferentiated, pure Consciousness. Like the seed, ātmā also has an intrinsic power. Because the seed and other worldly objects have a form, their power is limited. But Consciousness is formless. It permeates the entire world. Since It is Infinite, Its power is also Infinite. Unlike the seed which is insentient, Consciousness is sentient. The power of Consciousness is māyā. Māyā is that which measures and limits everything. It measures the Infinite Consciousness and presents it as though it is finite. Consciousness is not different from Its power. The power belongs to It. Hence, Consciousness Itself, by wielding Its own power, manifests as the phenomenal world.

Māyā first manifests as space and then as time. Time appears as matter. Space, time, and matter are the three dimensions of creation that even modern science accepts. They are the foundation stones for the entire creation. Space is formless and does not move. Time is formless but moves. Matter has form but does not move. Māyā creates these apparent divisions in the un-differentiated Consciousness. Like the combination of the seven basic colors to create different shades of colors or like the combination of the seven notes to create different melodies, these three dimensions of māyā combine together mysteriously to present the magical world we perceive.

Unlike the insentient power of the seed to sprout, māyā śakti, the power of Consciousness, is sentient. As a Conscious Power, it is Intelligence itself. It is aware of Its own expansion and manifestation because it is Awareness itself. It is the un-differentiated power of Consciousness Itself that appears as the manifested world.

According to logicians, the attributes of the cause appear in the effect. The world is the effect. Consciousness is the cause. Māyā śakti is the power that manifests the world out of Consciousness.

Although we refer to them as three (Consciousness, māyā, and the manifested world), in reality, these are not separate entities. The cause (Consciousness) itself manifests as the effect (world) through Its own creative power. The basic substance that the seed is made up of pervades the entire tree. Similarly, Consciousness Itself enters the creation and pervades it. From the viewpoint of the Absolute Reality, this means the entire creation is Consciousness alone, and the names and forms we perceive are only an appearance, a lie!

To illustrate this truth, Shankara provides two examples. The first is the example of a magician who hypnotizes his audience with his magical tricks. He manifests a beautiful city with celestial beings and wonderful objects. Mesmerized by his magic, people stare at his manifestations in wonder as though they are real. When the magician stops performing and withdraws his magical creations, nothing remains. He stands alone by himself. Where did all the objects he manifested come from and where did they disappear to? As long as he is performing, there are the magician, his magical powers, and the objects he manifests. When he stops performing and withdraws his manifestations, only he and his power remain. Since his power is not separate from him, he alone remains.

Shankara gives another analogy, the analogy of the great yogis of the past. A yogi's power is far greater than that of the magician. Ancient Indian mythologies are full of stories that describe the magnificent powers of great yogis. In Ramayana, for instance, Sage Bharadwaja is said to have manifested a delicious festive meal for King Bharata and his army in no time. In Mahabharata, when King Vishwamitra and his army arrived tired and hungry to Sage Vashista's hermitage, it is said that the sage received his guests with great respect and instantly served them a sumptuous meal with the help of his wish-fulling sacred cow (kāmadhenu). The king Vishwamitra, who later became Sage Vishwamitra, used his power of austerity to manifest a heaven in space! There are many such stories of different yogis at different times who displayed such great powers. Such yogis exist today as well, although we rarely see them.

How could these yogis demonstrate such great magical powers? What materials did they use? They did not require any external materials. They used their own inherent śakti (power) to manifest. Mere intention was enough to transform their knowledge (jñāna) into action (kriyā). They manifested objects and events according to people's wishes. The power of a yogi is not inert like the power of the seed. It is "Conscious power," so these yogis could manifest by mere intention. Inert objects, such as the seed, do not have such intrinsic sentient power. They depend on the universal all-pervading Conscious power to transform into anything, from a seed into a seedling, etc. The śakti of these inert objects, therefore, is limited, while the śakti of enlightened yogis is the Supreme Power of Consciousness, so It is unlimited.

Based on the extraordinary powers demonstrated by yogis, we can imagine the Infinite power of Supreme Consciousness. Since It is Complete and Perfect, Its power (māyā) is also Complete and Perfect. The world is the effect produced by the māyā śakti of the Supreme Consciousness. Śakti is not different from Consciousness.

Therefore, in reality, there is no world that is separate from Consciousness. The world we perceive is only a appearance of the creative-power (māyā*)* of Consciousness. Hence, the world is not different or separate from the power that manifested it, and the power is not different from the one who holds the power.

Verse 3. The Ever-Present "I Am" Awareness

yasyaiva sphuraṇaṃ sadātmakam asatkalpārthakaṃ bhāsate
sākṣāt tatvam asīti vedavacasā yo bōdhayatyāśritān ǀ
yassākṣātkaraṇād bhavenna punarāvṛttir bhavāmbhonidhau
tasmai śrīgurumūrtaye nama idaṃ śrī dakṣiṇāmūrtaye ǁ 3 ǁ

Consciousness is the cause and the world we perceive is the effect. The attributes of a cause pervade the effect. Therefore, the world cannot be different from the Consciousness. What are the attributes of the Consciousness that we see in the world? Shankara answers this question in this verse.

Consciousness is the spark of "I Am" awareness (sphuraṇa), the awareness of our own beingness or existence. Existence is *sat* and Awareness is *cit*. There can be no *sat* without *cit*, and no *cit* without *sat*. "I" must exist to be aware and "I" must be aware to know I exist. Existence-Awareness, *sat-cit*, are inseparable. Hence, Shankar uses a single phrase *sadātmākam* (Existence-Consciousness) to indicate the Oneness of the two aspects of Consciousness.

To whom or to what does this spark of Awareness (sadātmākam) belong? It belongs to that which can cognize its own existence. Only a sentient entity (ātmā) can cognize existence. Ātmā is sentient, so it is self-evident. Anātmā (world) is insentient, so it is not self-evident. An insentient entity cannot cognize its existence. Only a conscious being can cognize the objects of the external world and the thoughts and feelings of the internal world. Everything that is "known" to Consciousness is an "object" to Consciousness. Everything that is an object to Consciousness is anātmā

The awareness that "I Am" is real because it is present at all times. If it is absent sometimes, there would be nothing to cognize its absence. Cognition is possible only to Consciousness. One cannot deny one's own existence. The very fact that I think and am aware of my thoughts means I exist. Hence, the "I Am" Awareness, which is ever present, is the only Reality.

The world is anātmā. It has no cognition or awareness of its existence. It is not visible to itself, but it is visible to conscious beings like us. Anything that is perceived is not the Self. Self is formless Consciousness. It cannot be perceived like an object. Can Consciousness (ātmā) be aware of Itself? Like two lamps that cannot illumine each other, Consciousness cannot illumine itself because its very nature is Illumination! Senses cannot grasp ātmā. If it can be grasped by senses, it is anātmā. Our body, life-force, mind, and the world are all known to ātmā. Hence, they are anātmā (not-Self). Ātmā does not need anyone or anything to prove its existence.

The cause precedes the effect. Consciousness precedes the world. The attributes of the cause pervade the effect. Existence (sattā) and Consciousness (sphuraṇa*)* are the attributes of the Self. When our awareness (sphuraṇa) expands and pervades everything, the objects of the world become visible. If our awareness was confined to our body only and not expand, objects will not appear to us. Strictly speaking, the world is not even an appearance. It is our own Consciousness appearing as the mind, sense organs, names and forms.

Existence of the Self is the existence of the world. Existence does not have a definite form. The pot exists as clay. Similarly, the world exists as Existence-Consciousness. When we have a firm conviction that the Self alone IS, the external world will lose its separate identity. Along with the world, the upādhi-s or adjuncts through which the world is perceived, such as the body, mind, and life force, also lose their separateness. Upādhi-s perpetuate the feeling of a separate self (jīvā). When the upādhi-s disappear, the separate self also disappears. Two formless entities cannot exist separately. Just like two spaces, there cannot be two Consciousnesses. When there are no adjuncts to constrain it, the separate-self loses its separateness and merges into the Universal Self (Iśvara).

Consciousness is immediate and ever present. It is our innermost reality (pratyagātma). Because we wrongly associate our Self with our limited body-mind, we imagine that there is another larger, superior entity called Iśvara somewhere. This misconception disappears soon as we stop identifying with the body-mind.

Self is Pure Consciousness, but due to ignorance, we do not realize it. Knowledge dispels ignorance. When Knowledge of the Self arises and ignorance is destroyed, the all-pervasive Universal Consciousness reveals Itself as the Self. The triad - the individual, the world, and the creator - that once appeared as different entities, now dissolve into the Universal Consciousness. The cycle of birth and death is broken. The seeker no longer returns to saṃsāra because there is no longer a separate world to return to! When the jīvā and the jagat cease to exist as separate entities and Self alone remains as Pure Consciousness, the seeker experiences the great truth declared (mahāvākya) by the Upanishad *tat tvam asi* (You are That).

The mahāvākya, *tat tvam asi*, is an instructional statement. The mahāvākya *aham brahma asmi* is an experiential statement. An instruction precedes an experience. Only an accomplished teacher (sadguru) who has experienced the truth directly can provide such an instruction. Such a teacher is Lord Dakṣiṇāmūrti, the Supreme Consciousness Itself. He is the Guru of all gurus. Sitting under the banyan tree, surrounded by great sages like Vashista, one hand folded in cinmudra, the Lord is the ultimate instructor of *tat tvam asi*. The teacher-disciple tradition is based on this instruction. Guru is parabrahma. He who is established in Pure Consciousness and bestows the knowledge of the Self to his disciples is *brahman*.

Verse 4. Consciousness Illumines All

nanācchidra ghaṭodara sthita mahādīpa prabhā bhāsvaraṃ
jñānaṃ yasya tu cakṣurādikaraṇa dvārā bahiḥ spandate ǀ
jānāmīti tameva bhāntam anubhātyetatsamastaṃ jagat
tasmai śrī gurumūrtaye nama idaṃ śrī dakṣiṇāmūrtaye ǁ 4 ǁ

In the previous verse, Shankara established that the individual consciousness in our body is the same as the all-pervading Universal Consciousness. This is the truth declared by the mahāvākya *tat tvam asi*. Because the Consciousness referred to as 'you' (*tvam*) in the mahāvākya is already present in our body, we are able to say that the Consciousness in us is the same as 'That' (*tat*) Universal Consciousness. It is only with the help of the gross and the visible, we can infer the subtle and the invisible. If it were not so, our search for truth would be as baseless as trying to search for the snake that is no longer on the ground.

What we see is the body made up of five elements - earth, fire, water, wind, and space. Like the body, the sense organs are also made up of matter. The life-force (prāṇa), which helps the sense organs function together, constitutes the moving element called wind (vāyu). It enters the body and in the form of in-breath and out-breath, stays in close contact with the sense organs, and makes sure they are functioning. That is why prāṇa is called sūtra (string). Like a thread that strings together multiple beads, prāṇa strings together the five senses and their operations. Like the beads and the string, the senses and the lifeforce are all made up of matter.

While the nature of prāṇa is movement in the form of breath, the nature of mind is movement in the form of thoughts. Although prāṇa moves, it is not conscious. The mind moves but it is conscious.

Although the mind is conscious, it is not pure Consciousness. It is a false appearance of Consciousness. It is like an iron rod that becomes hot because of its long exposure to fire. If you touch the iron rod, it will burn your skin just like fire. However, iron is cold by nature and does not have the capacity to burn anything. Because of its close association with fire, it acquires the ability to burn. Hence, it is not exactly the iron rod that burns. It is the fire that burns through the medium called iron.

Similarly, Consciousness is not an attribute of the mind. Even though the mind generates thoughts endlessly, it is inert. The scripture says that the mind is a product of the food we eat. Food is of the nature of the earth element. The subtlest form of food becomes the mind and manifests as thoughts. Hence, everything, from the body to the mind, is made of the gross element earth. There is nothing other than the gross in the body.

In reality, there is no separate individual consciousness (jīvā caitanya). The "I Am" awareness that we experience is not different from the all-pervading Universal Consciousness. Several questions may arise at this point. Isn't it the mind that thinks "I see" "I act," etc., also think "I Am"? After all, isn't it the mind alone that is capable of thinking? Isn't the thought of "I Am" also an activity of the mind? If mind is made of matter just like the senses and other gross entities, wouldn't it also eventually dissolve into the five elements? If mind dissolves and all thoughts come to an end, wouldn't the thought of "I Am" also come to an end? If nothing remains upon the death of the body, where would that feeling of "I Am" be located? Even if we say there is Consciousness, isn't that also just a thought in the mind? Isn't it a fact that thoughts do not transcend the mind? Shankara addresses these questions now and establishes that awareness is not a product of the mind.

From the body to the mind, everything is made of inert matter. Since matter is insentient and not self-aware, there must be something else present to witness it. That witnessing entity is Consciousness. The witness is always distinct from the objects it witnesses, which includes the body, life-force, and mind.

It is easy to accept that the body and life-force are objects, but harder to accept that the mind is also an object. We think it is the mind that perceives everything. Mind is just a stream of thoughts. A thought is a movement (vṛtti) in the mind. Prior to the movement of thought, the mind is still. Consciousness is *acalam* (motionless). It is like an illumined screen on which objects appear like images. The images and the illumination together appear as a vṛtti, a thought-modification.

The images that appear on the screen (mind) are the objects of the world. If there are no objects, the screen would be empty. If it is empty, it is no longer the mind. It is the Self (ātmā). Ātmā, therefore, is distinct from the mind. It is Pure Consciousness in the form of illumination. It is due to the illumination supplied by Consciousness that the insentient mind appears as though a sentient entity. It (mind) is like the iron rod in the analogy we discussed earlier. Just like the iron rod which by nature is cool but becomes hot when it comes in contact with fire, so also the mind, which is originally insentient, appears as though sentient because of its contact with Consciousness.

Therefore, the Self is separate from the mind and life-force. Because It is sentient, It is Self-aware. Although the mind appears to be sentient, it borrows its sentience from Consciousness. While Consciousness is like a tranquil ocean, the mind is like a wave that rises from the ocean. Thoughts are like waves. When there is movement, there is a wave. When there is no movement, there is only water. Similarly, when Consciousness moves, it is the mind, and when it does not move it is ātmā. Although Consciousness appears to be in the body, it is not associated with it. It is like a lamp placed inside a pot with many holes. The light from the lamp flows out through the holes in the pot and illumines the pot, the holes, and the objects outside it.

Just because the lamp is inside the pot, the pot does not become the lamp. The lamp and the pot are separate entities. They are of different nature. The pot is of the nature of earth and the lamp is of the nature of fire. Whether the lamp is inside the pot or outside it, it can stand by itself as a lamp. Although the lamp appears as though inside the pot for the time-being, the pot is only an upādhi (adjunct). It does not hold the lamp in bondage. Moreover, the pot and everything around it are illumined by the lamp. They shine in the light of the lamp. The only relationship they (lamp and pot) have is that of "illumination" and the "illumined." Without illumination, objects do not appear. They depend on illumination to become visible. But the lamp itself does not depend on the objects. Whether or not the objects (upādhi-s) are present, the lamp shines on its own and makes other objects also shine it its presence.

Just like the lamp, Consciousness 'entered' the body. It did not actually "enter" the body. It only appears to have entered, just like the image that appears to have entered the mirror. Shining in its own effulgence, Consciousness flows out through our eyes, ears, and other sense organs to the world. The sense organs are like the holes in the pot. Consciousness flows out through them and illumines the moving and unmoving objects of the world around us. If it were not for the light of our Consciousness, the world would not appear to us. We would not even be aware of our own body, mind, and senses. If we are aware of our internal world (thoughts, emotions, etc.) and the external world, it is only because the light of our

Consciousness pervades everything. The light of Consciousness is not like the light of the lamp in the pot. Although separate from the pot, neither the lamp nor its light are sentient. They are both made up of gross elements. The lamp is not aware of its own effulgence or the fact that it is illumining the pot, etc. It is not self-aware. If it was self-aware, the lamp would be sentient. Therefore, although we refer to it as "light," the light of the lamp is not like the light of Consciousness. Consciousness is a light that is aware of everything. It is neither subjective nor objective. Even if the lamp is absent, the pot and objects around it continue to remain. However, if the light of Consciousness is absent, the world ceases to exist. Consciousness is both imminent and transcendent. Only because of Consciousness, the universe in its micro and macro forms appears to us. Without Consciousness, the universe will cease to exist.

For a thing to exist, there must be something that knows of its existence. Either the thing itself is aware of its existence or something else is aware of its existence. Without something or someone cognizing its existence, nothing can exist on its own. Whether the thing is aware of itself or something else is aware of it, it is only in awareness that the thing exists. Consciousness is the Witness, the proof of the existence of anything. For an object to exist, it must be "known" to Consciousness. The world and our body/mind are objects of knowledge to Consciousness. Therefore, only when Consciousness cognizes objects, we become aware of them. Hence, Existence means Knowability, and Knowability is the proof of Existence. Consciousness is the only proof of the existence of the world. We don't need to search for a proof to prove the existence of Consciousness. Since Its very nature is awareness, Consciousness is self-evident. Since it is self-evident, It is also self-existent. Unlike the pot and the lamp, Consciousness does not depend on anything for its existence.

Since it is self-evident, Consciousness is the only Real substance. Everything else that depends on It for its existence is unreal. If a thing comes into existence only when this other thing is present and ceases to exist when the other thing is absent, then that thing is not different from this other thing. They must be of the same intrinsic nature, just like the gold ornament that are not different from gold. Even when we see bracelets and necklaces, we only see gold. If we remove gold from the ornaments, the ornaments cease to exist.

Similarly, ātmā permeates everything. Just like the necklaces, bracelets, and other forms that gold appears in, Self as Consciousness appears as the body, mind, rivers, mountains, and other animate and inanimate objects. Although Consciousness appears to be inside the body, It pervades everything inside and outside the body. "I" shine as Awareness, and in "my" effulgence, everything shines. Consciousness is not 'in' the body, It IS the body. Hence, it can stand alone without any upādhi.

Verse 5. Misapprehensions about the Self

dehaṃ prāṇamapīndriyāṇyapi chalāṃ buddhiṃ ca śūnyaṃ viduḥ
strī bālāndha jaḍopamāstvahamiti bhrāntābhṛśaṃ vādinaḥ I
māyā śakti vilāsakalpita mahāvyāmoha saṃhāriṇe
tasmai śrī gurumūrtaye nama idaṃ śrī dakṣiṇāmūrtaye II 5 II

Using good reasoning and analogies, we have proved that Self alone Is Real. But this conclusion does not concur with our own experience or the experience of a common man or a brilliant scientist. From the materialists (cārvākā-*s*) to the Madhyamikā Buddhists (śūnya vāda-s or emptiness theorists), over ages, everyone one has enquired into the nature of Reality, and each came up with a different conclusion and doctrine.

Some concluded that the body is ātmā. Some thought the life-force is ātmā. Others thought the sense organs were ātmā. Those who consider the body, life-force, and sense organs as ātmā are the cārvākā-s or materialists They don't associate consciousness with ātmā. They think Self is an attribute of the body, mind, and sense organs. According to them, when the five elements combine and permutate in different proportions in the mind-body organism, a certain energy gets released. That energy according to them is ātmā or consciousness. It is like the feeling of intoxication that one experiences after drinking the fermented juice of the palm tree mixed together with molasses. That experience of intoxication is the result of the combination of different things. Each thing by itself would not produce such an effect.

Similarly, according to the materialists, the mixing up of the five elements in the different gross and subtle layers of our mind-body organism incidentally produces a conscious-energy in our body. The moment these elements separate and leave the body, the energy they generated will also dissipate. This is death. Therefore, materialists theorize that consciousness is a by-product of the mind-body organism, therefore it is not independent or separate from it.

The other type of theorists are the mind-only Buddhists (vijñāna vāda-s) and the Madhyamika Buddhists (śūnya vāda-s). The mind-only Buddhists assert that the mind is ātmā. They don't pause to think how can the mind that is born and dies every moment be the ātmā. The Madhyamika Buddhists, also known as the emptiness-theorists (śūnya vāda-s), on the other hand, argue that there is no mind, intellect, or ātmā anywhere, either inside us or outside us. All that is present is only space-like emptiness.

Although the proponents of all these doctrines appear as intellectuals and scientists, they are as good as common people who believe the same. None of them have a proper understanding of ātmā. They grasp whatever they can and call it ātmā. Not only are they confused, they also confuse others with their wrong understanding. Their vision and knowledge of reality is partial because they only see particulars and not the Universal. For Knowledge to be true, it must be complete. Partial knowledge is not true Knowledge.

To be called a scientist or an expert, knowledge must be complete. It cannot be limited, like the knowledge of a women, a child, or a blind man who have not been exposed to the world. The so-called intellectuals and scientists are just as confused as these people with limited knowledge. They don't see things as they really are. The fail to see the one and only substance that is ever present. Formless like space, Consciousness permeates everything. The names and forms we see appear in Consciousness. Like the gold and ornaments, Consciousness and the forms that appear in it are not different from each other.

But that is not how we perceive the world. We divide the formless Consciousness into parts and see spouse, children, homes, businesses, pain, pleasure, etc. Everything that we perceive is a form of Consciousness, but Consciousness is none of those forms. Forms are many, but Consciousness is One. Forms are fragments (divisible), but Consciousness is whole (undivided). Forms are of multiple types. But Consciousness is a single homogeneous substance.

A formless substance cannot be broken up into fragments. Doing so would be like a few blind men describing an elephant by touching one part of the elephant. Those who touch and feel its trunk only may think it is a pestle, those who feel its tail may think that it is a rope, those who feel its ears may think it is a sieve, and those who feel its legs may think it is a pillar. Each comes to a different conclusion about the name and form of the one entity because they mistook the parts for the whole. They were not capable of seeing the parts as a whole. If they did, they would have realized that there is only one entity, not several. Because they were touching and feeling parts, the one thing appeared as many.

Similarly, the one substance ātmā appears in multiple forms. We only see the forms It appears in, but fail to see the formless ātmā that pervades every form. Names and forms are the "parts" of the ātmā. However, unlike the parts that do not make up the entire elephant, ātmā is present in its entirety in the multitude of names and forms it appears in. Unlike the elephant which has a form, ātmā is formless awareness. It is indivisible. Because we only see names and forms, we reduce the formless ātmā to the forms we perceive. These forms are a manifestation of māyā, the creative power of Consciousness. So, they are not different from Consciousness. To grasp the formless, forms must dissolve. Unfortunately, instead of dissolving the forms into ātmā, we reduce ātmā to forms.

Our conception of the world is worse than the conception of the elephant by the blind men. Instead of mistaking the part for the whole as the blind men did, we mistake the entire world (anātma) for ātma. Shankara calls this the greatest misconception *(mahāvyāmoha)*. This misapprehension of what is Real has haunted us for life times. Shankara says we are deluded by māyā. The intrinsic creative power of Consciousness has the capacity to make Consciousness appear limited. Consciousness is Infinite and cannot be constrained. Like the mighty sun that is hidden by a passing cloud, Consciousness is hidden by illusory forms.

Due to the veiling power of māya, Pure Consciousness appears as though fragmented into time, space, and the world. It is our great misfortune that, due to ignorance, we see finite forms instead of the Absolute Reality. For Absolute Reality to shine, ignorance must be removed.

Who can remove ignorance? The creator (Iśvara) or the individual (jīva)? Only Iśvara can remove ignorance. If we were capable of doing so ourselves, we would have done so long ago and be liberated from samsara. Because Iśvara is omnipotent, He is called Iśvara, the Controller. Although He holds us in bondage with His māyā power, He is also compassionate and capable of releasing us from bondage. He has the power to pull us out of saṃsāra or push us deeper into it. "Pushing down" is to keep us trapped in the cycle of birth and death. "Pulling out" is to equip us with Self-Knowledge so that we can break the cycle of birth and death. This is the meaning of the line in the third verse - *sākṣāt tat tvam asi*.

The Lord Dakṣiṇāmūrti, sitting under the banyan tree, silently transmitting Self-Knowledge to his disciples, is Consciousness Itself. Every great teacher of Self-Knowledge is the Lord Himself.

Guru is *brahman*. When disciples receive the Knowledge of the Self from an enlightened teacher and realize the teaching, they too become *brahman*, just like their teacher. Only Knowledge received from an eminent teacher can liberate a seeker. It is sheer grace that we are receiving this Knowledge. Our responsibility is to contemplate and actualize that Knowledge. Our own sincere efforts together with the grace of the Guru will remove the thick veil of darkness or ignorance that has enveloped us. Once the veil of ignorance is removed, we will immediately experience our true Self as Pure Consciousness.

Verse 6. Ignorance Eclipses Knowledge

rāhugrasta divākarendu sadṛśo māyā samācchādanāt
sanmātraḥ karaṇōpa saṃharaṇato yo'bhūtsuṣuptaḥ pumān ǀ
prāgasvāpsamiti prabodha samaye yaḥ pratyabhijñāyate
tasmai śrī gurumūrtaye nama idaṃ śrī dakṣiṇāmūrtaye ǁ 6 ǁ

Why should we make the effort to get rid of anātmā? Can't anātmā disappear by itself as it does in deep sleep? During waking and dream states we have the sense of 'I' and of the object 'I' see. But in deep sleep we do not have that sense of I-ness. We are not aware of either the external or the internal world. Even our thoughts disappear in deep sleep. Ātmā alone Is. If ātmā alone Is, why are we not aware of It in deep sleep? If ātmā is Consciousness Itself, shouldn't it be aware of Itself even in deep sleep? Does ātmā disappear along with anātmā in deep sleep? These are the questions that Shankara addresses in this verse.

Even if the body, mind, and external world disappear in deep sleep and it appears as though there is nothing, there certainly ***is*** something. It is not the gross body or the subtle mind. It is the causal body, which is subtler than the mind. While the gross body and mind are dormant in deep sleep, the causal body is active and present like a thick curtain of darkness.

We can grasp the gross body (annamaya kośa) and mind (manomaya kośa) because they are visible to us, but we cannot grasp the causal body because it is extremely subtle and invisible. A body is a collection of gross and subtle parts. The mind is subtler than the gross body, so it is called the subtle body (manomaya kośa). Whatever shrouds the Infinite Consciousness and makes it appear finite is a body (śarīra). Just like the gross body and mind which cover the Infinite Consciousness and make It appear finite, so also does the causal body. The causal body is made up of vāsanā-s, which are the deep impressions in the mind. The mind is like a piece of cloth wrapped around the spice called asafetida. Even after removing the spice, however hard we try, we will not be able to wash away the pungent smell of the spice from the cloth. Tendencies or impressions in the mind are like the lingering smell of the spice in the cloth. Over life-times, we have accumulated many deep impressions (vāsanā-s) that persist in the causal body.

So strong and many are these vāsanā-s that they persist even after the mind and the world subside (as in deep sleep or death of the body). Transactions with the world generate thought-modifications (vṛtti-s), which in turn create deep binding impressions. These deep-rooted impressions constitute māyā, avidyā, or nescience. Advaita refers to these tendencies as the causal body because it is the reason for rebirth and the need for a body to continue to satisfy desires. Since its very nature is avidyā, the causal body persists until one attains vidyā, Self-Knowledge. Attaining Self-Knowledge means realizing that Self alone IS, and everything that is perceived is only an appearance of the Self. Just like the darkness that is dispelled upon sunrise, the moment the Knowledge of the Self rises in the individual, nescience is dispelled. This is liberation. Until we attain such Knowledge and be liberated, we will continue to suffer the consequences of the causal body as saṃsāra.

Even though we are not aware of our body-mind and the external world in deep sleep, we do not experience real peace, which is our true nature, because our causal bodies continue to be active. Just like the effulgence of the sun and the moon that is temporarily eclipsed by the shadow of the earth, the ever-shining Consciousness (ātmā) is present, but temporarily hidden by ignorance in deep sleep.

Ātmā (Self) is ever present as Existence-Consciousness. Existence and Consciousness are not two separate things. They are one and the same. Where Existence Is, Awareness Is. This is an irrevocable principle of Advaita. Awareness appears as though absent in deep sleep because the sense organs and the mind are defunct. The instrument called mind is not present to comprehend the 'nothingness,' the absence of objects and thoughts, in deep sleep. When the cognizing instrument is not available, there is no knowledge of anything. Hence, Consciousness appears as though absent in deep sleep.

A question may be raised here. If Consciousness is ever present and is Self-Aware, why does It dependent on the mind and sense organs for Its existence? Due to habituated wrong thinking we think it is only through our mind that we know we exist. We forget that our Self transcends the mind. We think that we exist because our minds exist and cease to exist if our minds cease to exist. Truth is that the I-Am awareness that the mind cognizes transcends the mind. Consciousness (Self) does not depend on anything for its existence. Because we lack the knowledge that Self is the ever-present Consciousness, we assume Self is absent when the mind and sense organs are absent in deep sleep.

In deep sleep, there is no mind to cognize the Self, even though the Self is present as *sat-cit*, Existence and Consciousness. Even if the mind is absent, Consciousness is aware. Even in deep sleep, there is no gap in Its awareness. It's effulgence remains undiminished. The mind is only an instrument through which Consciousness manifests externally. Just because the image of an object appears in the mirror, we cannot assume that the mirror created the object. Whether or not the image appears in the mirror, the object can stand on its own. The mirror is only a projector, not the creator of the object. Similarly, mind is just a projecting instrument. Even if the mind is defunct, there is no problem. Consciousness continues to shine on Its own.

If Consciousness is present only when the mind is present and is totally absent in deep sleep, we will not be aware of It on waking up. It is not possible to remember something suddenly without having experienced it previously. Cognition and experience precede memory. This is common experience.

On waking up, we remember our experience of having slept peacefully the night before. If we were not aware of the peace we experienced in deep sleep, how would we remember it on waking up? Having experienced something, we recollect it. Therefore, even in deep sleep, Self is aware. If there is a break in the Self, in our Consciousness, we would cease to exist in deep asleep and suddenly come back into existence on waking up. As Sri Krishna says in Bhagavad Gita (2-16), "That which exists does not cease to exist, and that which does not exist, does not come into existence. What IS does not disappear suddenly."

Consciousness is the intuitive awareness that "I Am." It is our essential nature, so it can never be absent. If It is present sometimes and absent at other times, it cannot be our essential nature. If Consciousness is absent, we will be absent as well. Consciousness must be present to even cognize its absence! Saying "Consciousness is absent" is as ridiculous as saying "I have no tongue."

Therefore, the ātmā is present in the waking, dream, and deep-sleep states as Existence and Consciousness. Only because the instrument called mind is temporarily defunct in deep sleep, we think ātmā is absent. However, if ātmā is really absent in deep sleep, we would have no recollection (pratyabhigna) after waking up of having slept soundly. Unless there is cognition of something, there can be no recognition, recollection, or memory of it.

When we meet someone after a long time, we recognize them because of our past experience with them, even though we have lost touch with them in between. Even if we did not experience them directly during the gap, they were present and experiencing themselves all the time. That is why, we were able to recognize them again later when we see them. As the scripture puts it, "*so 'yam Devadattaḥ,*" "This is that same Devadatta that I saw in the past." We are able to recognize someone or something based on our past experience because there is no difference between the thing of the past and the thing of the present. They are one and the same. The difference is only in time and place, not in the essential nature of the thing itself.

We must apply the same logic to our deep sleep experience. It is the same Self, Consciousness, that was present before we went to sleep and that is present after we wake up. In the middle, during deep sleep, Consciousness appears to be temporarily absent (anupalabdhi), not annihilated, because the mind that cognizes the presence and absence of objects is absent. If Self were to be completely annihilated in deep sleep, we would have no memory or recognition of ourselves after we wake up. When "I" go to sleep, it is the same "I" that wakes up. No one else wakes up in my place. Therefore, it is clear that in the waking, dream, and deep sleep states, Self, is in no way diminished. It shines without a break.

If it appears as though the Self is absent at times, like the sun during eclipse, we must remind ourselves that the Self is the "I Am" awareness that is ever present. This recollection of that ever shining awareness of the Self is *pratyabhigna*. This in essence is the purport of the sixth verse.

Verse 7. Self is Immutable

bālyadiṣvapi jāgradādiṣu tathā sarvāsv avasthāsvapi
vyāvṛttasv anuvartamānam aham ityantaḥ sphurantaṃ sadā ।
svātmānaṃ prakaṭikaroti bhajatāṃ yo mudrayā bhadrayā
tasmai śrī gurumūrtaye nama idaṃ śrī dakṣiṇāmūrtaye ॥ 7 ॥

Pratyabhigna is the recognition of that which is ever-present. As long as we can recognize a thing from past experience, we can assert that that the thing really exists. If there is no opportunity for pratyabhigna (recognition), then the thing does not exist. The substance that is always present in both ātmā and anātmā (Self and not-Self) is Consciousness. The world (not-Self) appears in the waking states but disappears in deep sleep. What is real must exist at all times. Since, we do not experience the world at all times in all states, it is unreal. Even though it is unreal, we continue to see the world because we fail to see the ever-present Self. Our vision is superficial. Only when our vision is expansive and penetrating, we will be able to separate the Real from the unreal. Pratyabhigna can be of great help in this regard.

Shankara now explains how to enquire into the nature of Reality. He says change is constant. Childhood changes into youth, youth changes into old age, and old age changes into death. The waking state changes to dream state, the dream state changes to deep sleep state, and the deep sleep state changes to waking state. Our experience in the waking state changes minute to minute. We are happy one minute and sad the next. We are brave one minute and cowardly the next. From birth to death, change is constant. Nothing is stable. Emotions, feelings, situations change constantly. This is called vyāvṛtti, discontinuity. There is no continuity or scope for pratyabhignya in the ever-changing world. Although it appears as though there is continuity, if we look deeply, we will realize the impermanent nature of the world. We don't need the scripture to tell us that. Situations and events from the past appear as dreams to us in the present. Dreams are unreal.

The opposite of vyāvṛtti is anuvṛtti (continuity). Even when childhood, youth, and events keep changing, the pulsating awareness that "I Am" continues without a break. This persisting feeling of "I-Am-ness" gives scope to pratyabhignya. Whatever gives scope for pratyabhigna is Real. While states change (vyāvṛtti), Consciousness remains changeless (anuvṛtti). We are aware of its unchanging nature in every changing situation. Childhood has gone and youth has arrived. But I Am. Youth has gone and old age has arrived, but I still am. Old age has gone and death has arrived, but I remain. It is the same "I" that experienced youth and old age that is now experiencing death. Through all these changes, my real nature as Consciousness remains. This constant awareness is pratyabighna. Since I am always aware of my Self through all changing states, my Self can never undergo any harm.

A question arises at this point. Does the Self die when the body and mind die? Is there an opportunity for pratyabhigna at the time of death? Since the I-Am Awareness is ever-present, It must be present even at the time of death. If not, who is to experience death? There must be something present to experience death. Death cannot experience itself. All experience is only to Consciousness. It is Consciousness Itself that has experienced childhood, youth, and old age. It must be Consciousness Itself that also experiences the death of the body. Wherever there is experience, Consciousness must be present. If Consciousness is present, that means the Self is present. Therefore, Self cannot be destroyed. As the scripture declares, the Self is *avināśi*, indestructible.

Self is ātmā. It is the me-ness, the sense of "I Am" that is ever present. While others may not cognize our 'I-Am-ness', we should be able to cognize It because it is our very own Self. Yet we do not cognize our real Self! We only cognize the false self, and not the Real Self. If we truly grasp the Real Self, we will stop seeing the not-Self. When we clearly see the rope, we will stop seeing a snake in its place. If we continue to see the snake, instead of the rope, that means we have not seen the rope clearly. Similarly, once we have completely realized the true nature of the Self, we will stop seeing the not-Self (world). But in the waking state, along with the feeling of "me-ness," we also have the feeling of "mine" because we see the world and transact with it as 'mine.' Therefore, the 'I-Am' awareness we have in the waking state is not the real Self because it is not pure objectless Awareness.

This false sense of self, however, can lead us to the Real Self. It is like the shadow of a pigeon on the ground. Even though the shadow is only a false appearance, it can help us locate the real pigeon in the sky. Once we grasp the real pigeon, we can ignore the shadow. It has served its purpose. Similarly, this pulsating feeling of I-Am-ness that we experience is like the shadow of the pigeon. It is not the real Self. It is the ego, a shadow of the Real Self. Since it is the ego that transacts with the world, we think it is the real self, even though it is very limited. Hence, Advaita refers to it as anātmā or not-self. As long as we identify with the body, mind, and sense organs and think we are the doers and enjoyers of our actions, we identify with the active self (ego), not the passive witnessing Self. To remain as Pure Awareness, there can be no feeling of "me" or "mine." The not-self (world) must merge completely into the Self to experience Self as Pure Consciousness.

To realize the true nature of the Self, Advaita prescribes the practice of śravaṇa (listen) and manana (contemplate) continuously.

We need an eminent teacher to help us in our practice. When great sayings of the Upanishads, such as *tat tvam asi,* are taught by an enlightened teacher to a disciple, and if the disciple contemplates on the teaching, the disciple too will realize the Self. When that realization takes place, the knowledge of the Infinite that has been lying dormant in the disciple will awaken and blossom. Great teachers (ācārya-s) appear on earth from time to time to reveal this profound Knowledge to sincere seekers who are devoted to the Truth. Lord Dakṣiṇāmūrti, the foremost of all such teachers, reveals the Truth in silence using a jñāna *mudra.*

A mudra is an external symbol that points to an internal truth. If the internal truth is not grasped, the symbol will remain a symbol, and the truth that it is pointing to will be lost. Once the truth is grasped, the symbol can be discarded. Khecarī, bhūcari, and other yoga mudras are all such symbols. However, the aim of yoga mudras is prosperity (preyas), not peace (śreyas). Śreyas is mokṣa or freedom from saṃsāra. The jñāna mudra indicates śreyas because it points to Knowledge. It is also called the cinmudra – the joining of the thumb with the index finger of the right hand. The index finger represents the individual who enters the world and identifies with it. The three fingers next to the index finger represent the three qualities or guṇa-s (rajas, tamas, and satva) that the body, mind, and the world are made up of. As long as we are totally identified with the guṇa-s, we will have no awareness of the Self. To get a firm grasp on the Self, we must distance ourselves from the guṇa-s. The thumb represents the Supreme Self or Consciousness. The thumb joined with the index finger symbolizes the union of the individual self with the Supreme Self. When the individual self merges into the Supreme Self, the not-Self (world) loses its separate identity. Everything is experienced as one's own Infinite Self. This in essence is the meaning of the seventh verse.

Verse 8. Cause Manifests as the Effect

viśvaṃ paśyati kāryakāraṇatayā svasvāmi sambandhataḥ
śiṣya ācāryatayā tathaiva pitṛ putrādyātmanā bhedataḥ ।
svapnē jāgrati vā ya eṣa puruṣo māyā paribhrāmitaḥ
tasmai śrī gurumūrtaye nama idaṃ śrī dakṣiṇāmūrtaye ॥ 8 ॥

While it is possible to experience the Self since it is our own nature, it is not a common experience. If it is a common experience, whoever has been hearing the teaching for a long time would have experienced the Self by now. But that is not what we see in the world. Shankara reminds us about the power of māyā in this verse. Māyā manifests in two ways in our lives: as the contracting or veiling power and the distracting or projecting power. With its veiling power, māyā limits the Infinite Self and makes it appear as the finite self. With its projecting power, māyā hides what is real (Consciousness) and projects the unreal (world). Therefore, we suffer in two ways.

These veiling and projecting powers of māyā bind us in saṃsāra. Although, we are aware of our self, our awareness is not complete or perfect. It is constricted because of our identification with the adjuncts (body, mind, and sense organs), and not the Pure Self. Hence, in our conventional understanding, the self we know is the false self (separate self). It is this limited self only that we experience throughout our life. We experience the three states (awake, dream, deep sleep) one after the other endlessly. In the waking state, the awareness or sense of "I" is prominent. In the dream state, that awareness is vague. In deep sleep, it is completely gone. What is the use of such awareness if it is present sometimes and not at other times? Even if it is present in the waking and dream state, of what use is it if it is not the awareness of the real Self? We are not able to free ourselves from the bondage of the not-Self. Therefore, the real

Self remains hidden in all three states. The contracting power of māyā reigns over the deep sleep and the projecting power of māyā reigns over the waking and dream states. Shankara refers to these different powers in the sixth and eight verses. In the sixth verse, he refers to the veiling power of māyā (*āchādana*) in the deep sleep state. In the eighth verse, he refers to the projecting power of māyā (*paribhrāmitaḥ*) in the waking and dream states.

When the veiling power of māyā operates, Infinite Consciousness appears as a finite self with a distorted vision, just like the distorted vision of a child who is spun around by two hands. Under the spell of the projecting power of māyā, our vision gets distorted and we see the unreal as real. In the waking and dream states, we see objects and not the underlying reality in which they appear.

We enjoy this magical world and the pleasures and pains it offers, but we are also curious about its real nature. To realize the true nature of the world and the Self, we need an eminent teacher, an ācārya who has attained Self-Knowledge and is capable of transmitting the Knowledge to us. A true disciple is one who can grasp the Knowledge "as is" from an ācārya. It is this teacher-disciple tradition that keeps the lamp of Self-Knowledge lit and shining through the ages. Since it helps seekers in their search for truth, the teacher-disciple relationship is considered to be the most important relationship in the world.

All relationships in the world can be summed up as cause and effect relationships. However, the cause is not different from the effect. In the father-son relationship, for instance, he who is a son with reference to his father, is a father with reference to his son.

This entire creation is like a magical production. It is through the creative power or śakti of the magician (Supreme Self) that the world with its moving and unmoving objects is projected. Hence, the Supreme Self is the cause for the appearance of the world. In the dream and waking states, we perceive a world of objects. We perceive the objects (effect) as different from the source or cause. This is due to a dualistic vision that fails to see the cause that permeates the effect (world). It is the Supreme Self, Consciousness, Itself that appears as the world. When we forget the non-dual nature of our Self, we see multiplicity not unity. We perceive the world as "mine" and ourselves as its owners. We assume a "me and mine" relationship with the world and get deeply entrenched in it. We ascribe a cause and effect relationship to the Lord and His creation and a "me and mine" relationship to ourselves and the world.

It is this me-mine relationship with the world that leads to bondage (saṃsāra). The vision that sees duality fails to grasp the underlying unity. It does not have the non-dual understanding that it is the cause itself that is appearing as the effect. This misapprehension and perception of the unreal as real is māyā.

Verse 9. Recognizing the Cause in the Effect

bhūr ambhāṃsyanalo 'nilo'mbaram aharnātho himānśuḥ pumān
ityābhāti carācarātmakam idaṃ yasyaiva mūrtyaṣṭakam |
nānyat kiñcana vidyate vimṛśatāṃ yasmāt parasmād vibhoh
tasmai śrī gurumūrtaye nama idaṃ śrī dakṣiṇāmūrtaye || 9 ||

Therefore, all misapprehensions are due to māyā. But this is only a diagnosis of the disease, not a cure. Every disease has a corresponding cure. If we keep talking about the disease without talking about a cure, it is a waste of time. The problem will remain a problem. We have established so far that saṃsāra (the cycle of birth and death) is the problem and māyā is the source of the problem.

Shankara is providing a solution to the problem in this verse. The first step in solving any problem is to understand the context in which the problem occurs. The second step is to find the source or cause of the problem. The final step is to solve the problem. The problem will then transform into a solution.

The snake-rope example is a good analogy to explain this situation. On a twilight evening, we see something that appears like a snake on the ground and we are frightened. What we see is actually a rope, not a snake, but we didn't know that initially. The rope appeared as a snake and frightened us. That means the cause (rope) itself appeared as the effect (snake). We have to investigate the cause to clearly understand the source of the problem and find a solution. This is the first step. If we flash a light and investigate, we will find a rope, not a snake. Seeing the rope is identifying the cause. This is the second step in solving the problem. Once we acquire the knowledge of the rope, what appeared as a snake earlier, will now appear as a rope. The form of the snake disappears into the rope. This is the third step – the solution to the problem. The rope appearing as a snake is the problem. The rope appearing as a rope is the solution.

Since it is the rope itself (kāraṇa/cause) that appeared as a snake (kriyā/manifestation), the moment we have the knowledge of the rope, the illusory snake disappears into the rope. Not all effects in the world, however, merge so smoothly into the cause. For instance, in the case of the gold ornaments, gold is the cause and the ornaments are the effects. Although we see the gold, unlike the snake in the rope analogy, the ornaments do not disappear into the gold. We continue to see necklaces, rings, etc. along with the gold. To make the ornaments disappear altogether, we need to make the additional effort of melting the ornaments into gold.

It is in such circumstances that Shankara suggests we apply the power of pratyabhigna (recognition). When we look deep into the effect, we will realize that it is the cause or substance itself that is appearing as the effect. It is this recognition of the common and constant factor in every form that is called pratyabhigna. Although we call it an 'effect,' the truth is, there is no separate entity as an 'effect' because it is the cause itself that appears as the effect. Shankara refers to the effect as saṃsthānāṃ (formation). A block of ice floating on water is a formation of water. When we see any formation of water, even without melting it, we recognize immediately that it is water. Water can appear in a solid or a liquid form. The liquid form is its intrinsic nature. The solid form is its appearance (vibhūti). An 'effect' is the expansion of the cause, which is the real substance.

Therefore, an effect is nothing but the cause itself. It appears as an effect because the cause manifests in a form, instead of remaining in its intrinsic formless nature. The form or the effect veils or hides the original nature of the cause. Not only does the form make it difficult for us to see or recognize the real substance, it also creates the illusion that the form itself is real! As a result, our vision gets trapped in the illusion of the form, and fails to penetrate into the substance that pervades the form. If our vision is capable of penetrating to the substance, we would recognize the truth that the form is not different from the substance. But we do not have such a vision or experience.

Such a vision and experience is possible through pratyabhigna. Since the effect (world) has emerged from the cause, which is our very intrinsic nature (Self), the effect is not different from the cause. Whenever we perceive the effect, we must remember the cause. This recollection of our original nature is pratyabhigna. Pratyabhigna is the only sādhana (practice) required in Advaita.

There is no other effort required, since there is nothing new to attain. There is also no need to associate the Self with any object in order to see It. It is Self-evident (*svataḥ siddha*). Consciousness is its very form. Whatever form we imagine, it is only Consciousness appearing in that form. Therefore, rituals and actions are useless in realizing the Self. Knowledge of the Self is the only requirement.

We are capable of seeing the Absolute Truth. But we got used to seeing multiplicity. This makes us think we are in bondage. To be free of this feeling of bondage, we must divert our attention to the underlying Consciousness that permeates every object we see in the world. When our attention is focused on the common substance that permeates all objects, objects will lose their separateness and merge into Consciousness. Since Consciousness is the very nature of the Self, the cause and effect that appeared as separate entities earlier, will now be experienced as the Self.

The function of pratyabhigna is to engender that harmonious experience of the Self. The first step in the process is to perceive the effect objectively. The next step is to use pratyabhigna to recognize the cause that produced the effect. The final step is to see the cause itself as the effect. As Advaita practitioners, we must contemplate and practice this relentlessly, until the object world completely melts away and what remains is Pure Consciousness alone.

Shankara is elucidating on this practice when he says, "bhūr ambhāṃsy analō' nilōmbaram aharnāthō himāṃśuḥ pumān." *bhū* means earth, *ambhās* means water, *analah* means fire, *anilah* means wind, and *ambaram* means space. These are the five elements that make up the world. Shankara adds three more to the list – *aharnātha, himānsu, and pumān*. In the conventional sense, *aharnātha* refers to the sun, *himānsu* refers to moon, and *pumān* refers to man or the landlord. These are the literal meanings or primary interpretations of the words and the sentence. However, such an interpretation is not appropriate in this context because, the sun, moon, and the human body are included in five elements. Why did Shankara specifically mention the sun, moon, and human body?

We must go beyond the primary meaning of this sentence to understand the real intent of Shankara. Metaphorically speaking, the three entities (sun, moon, man) represent the mind, intellect, and ego respectively. This explanation corresponds to the Chapter 7, verse 4 in Bhagavad Gita, where Sage Vyasa describes the six-fold creation (nature) of Iśvara, and explicitly mentions mind, intellect, and ego along with the five elements. It is this same concept that Shankara describes in this verse using symbolic terms.

While the five elements denote the external world, the remaining three entities (mind, intellect, and ego) denote the internal world of the human being. Together these eight entities are called *aṣṭamūrti*-s. This entire creation is a manifestation of these eight entities. They appear inside us as thoughts and feelings and outside us as names and forms. They are the source of the problem.

Shankara now provides a solution to the problem. He says, the myriad forms we perceive externally are the manifestations of the formless Consciousness. By making that statement, he merges the not-Self into the Self. When we hear those words, our vision which has been narrowly focused on objects, expands to focus on the all-pervading Consciousness, the source from which the world manifests. Up until now, our eyes have been perceiving only the effect, and not the cause. By pointing to the cause that is hidden in the effect, Shankara draws the cause out to the forefront. When our attention is drawn to the cause, Consciousness flashes in our mind together with the world that our senses perceive.

We have spent most of our life seeing names and forms, and not the source from which they appear. Hence our vision is deluded. The more we focus and engage with objects, the more we suffer under their pressure. If we view the objects in association with the Consciousness in which they appear, they will have less impact on us. Consciousness is a single Undifferentiated and Formless substance. The world is a fragmented collection of forms. When our vision is on the formless substance, forms dissolve into the formless substance. Mind becomes lighter and capable of glossing over names and forms, instead of getting weighed down by them. Free of names and forms, the mind will automatically break free of bondage. This is the second step in the practice – to focus on the cause and not on the effect.

The third and last step in the practice is to merge the effect (world) into the cause. As long as we see duality, we are in bondage. How can we attain liberation? Shankara says, *nānyatkiñchana vidyatē vimṛśatāṃ yasmātparasmādvibhō* – those who investigate deeply will find no difference between the cause and the effect. They will see everything as the Self, the spark of "I Am" awareness (sadātmākam, sphuraṇa) that pervades everything.

We must contemplate deeply on this spark of Awareness. We must touch and feel it in every animate and inanimate object we perceive, just as we touch and feel an object with our hand. What is the common factor that is present in every object? Existence and Consciousness (sattā and sphuraṇa). Presence and Awareness (*sat* and *cit*). Every object we perceive in this world has these two common qualities. The pot exists (is) and I Am Aware of its existence. The painting exists and I am aware of its existence. Presence and Awareness is the essence of everything in this world. We wonder how this can be true because the world appears full of polarities - thin-fat, long-short, black-white, good-bad, positive-negative. When there are so many differences in the objects, how can we say that presence-awareness (sat-cit) is the only basic attribute of all objects? Yes, it is true that there are many differences between objects. But, as practitioners of Advaita, if we pay close attention to just these two common qualities, we would be paying attention to all the attributes. We don't have to look at each attribute separately because, whatever attribute we look at, it simply "is" (*sat*) and we are aware (*cit*) of its "is-ness."

When our focus is on the Universal, particulars dissolve into the Universal. Because particulars originally manifested from the Universal, they are not different from the Universal. Therefore, when we perceive objects from the viewpoint of the Universal, they will appear as the Universal. When we view ornaments as gold, they will appear as gold. Similarly, when we view the world from the viewpoint of the Universal, all moving and unmoving objects of the world will appear as Pure Consciousness. Because Consciousness appears in different forms, we think that Consciousness (cause) and world (effect) are separate entities. When we investigate deeply into the cause and the effect, we stop seeing them as separate things. Even the very words "cause and effect" become meaningless, since they are both relative and interdependent concepts. If one is absent, the other is absent too. To a homogenous vision, the two appear as One. A "vision" is not different from the "visionary." Hence, everything (subject and object) dissolve in the One Universal Self.

Verse 10. Sarvātmabhāva - the Fruit of Advaita Sadhana

sarvātmatvam iti sphuṭīkṛtam idaṃ yasmād amuṣmin stave
tenāsya śravaṇāt tadartha mananād dhyānāt ca saṅkīrtanāt I
sarvātmatva mahā vibhūti sahitaṃ syād īśvaratvaṃ svataḥ
siddhyet tatpunar aṣṭadhā pariṇataṃ ca iśvaryam -avyāhatam II 10 II

This verse describes the nature of the Universal Self. In the last nine verses as well, Shankara has repeatedly discussed this very subject. In the first three verses, he established that the apparent world is unreal. In the next three verses, he established the non-difference of Iśvara (Creator) and jīvā (individual). In the seventh verse, he explained that that the Self alone is Real and the not-Self is unreal. In the eighth verse, he explained how ātmā is incorrectly associated with anātmā, and how this association perpetuates the disease called saṃsāra. In the ninth verse, he provided a solution to free us from saṃsāra.

Shankara used the word *vimṛśatāṃ* in the ninth verse. This is a gem of a word. Hidden in it are several clues that can help a seeker in his or her practice (sādhana). Since it is difficult for seekers to grasp the teaching if it is buried too deep, Shankara elaborates on the teaching in this verse. He describes the process of self-enquiry and the fruit of such a practice. The fruit is *sarvātma bhāva*, a state of being in identity with All. An unbroken seamless Oneness.

To attain such a state of Oneness, a sincere seeker must mediate deeply on this teaching. Shankara suggests a three-step practice: śravaṇa, manana, and nididhyāsana. The first step, śravaṇa, is to read the scripture or listen to an experienced teacher with devotion and commitment to know the truth. This requires an in-depth understanding of the meaning of each word in an Upanishadic statement and a comprehensive understanding of the entire sentence. For instance, in the mahāvākya *tat tvam as*i (That Thou Art), the student must first understand the meaning of each word in the sentence - *tat, tvam,* and *asi,* and later integrate them all to get a comprehensive understanding of the entire sentence. Only when we have such an in-depth and comprehensive understanding of the sentence, we will realize that the words *tat* and *tvam* are pointing to the same thing. Such knowledge removes ignorance. The seeker realizes that ātmā, pure Consciousness, permeates and transcends Iśvara and jagat.

In spite of having a good understanding of the truth, we find it difficult to separate ātmā (Self) from anātmā (world). We continue to be confused about the relationship of the insentient world with the Consciousness which is our very nature. Are they the same or are they separate? To really understand the teaching and make it our experience, just śravaṇa is not enough. Manana or deep contemplation on the teaching is essential. With the help of the reasoning and analogies provided by the scripture and the teacher, we must clearly understand that the effect (world) is not separate from the cause (Consciousness), even though it appears as though it is different.

Intellectual knowledge of the Self must mature into a firm conviction. Without firm conviction in the teaching, knowledge will disappear the moment the world appears. The Self will once again appear as Not-Self. This is viparyaya, misapprehension. When a thing appears in reverse, as something different from what it really is, it is viparyaya. That means, instead of the world appearing as Existence-Consciousness, it appears as names and forms. What is the use of manana if our conviction is so weak that it gets shaken with the least challenge? We will be like the elephant that rolls itself in dirt right after it takes a dip in the river. To develop firm conviction that the Self Alone Is, manana must culminate in nididhyāsana - deep, prolonged, uninterrupted meditation on the Self (Existence-Consciousness). Like the salt present in every drop of salt water, Consciousness is present in everything. We cannot see the salt in the water with our eyes or feel it with our hands. We can only taste it with our tongue. Similarly, when our vision is focused only on the common substance that permeates all particulars, we will experience the common substance, not the particulars.

A vision that only sees particulars is a fragmented vision. The vision that can see the common substance that permeates all particulars is a homogenous vision. When our vision is continuously focused on the Self alone, like the uninterrupted flow of oil, it is called nididhyāsana. Whatever we see, hear, or think in this world, we must remind ourselves, "It is my Self alone, Pure Existence-Consciousness, that appears to me the seer, as though molded, folded, and solidified into these wonderous forms of the world." If we train our minds to perceive everything as nothing other than the Self, gradually particulars will lose their specificity and dissolve into the Universal. Forms become blurred and everything that was earlier experienced as particulars will now be experienced as the Universal Self. Since the vision is on the Universal and not on the particulars, there is no duality. Duality in the form of likes and dislikes, good and bad vanishes. There is no more saṃsāra (bondage). Only sāyujya, liberation. When we attain this state of being, there will be no difference between transcending (samādhi) the world or transacting with it. Even if it appears as though we are transacting with the world, we will feel that we have transcended it. Life becomes samādhi. In the beginning, in ignorance, we experienced life as eternal bondage, but now, in Knowledge, we experience life as eternal liberation.

When everything is experienced as the Self (sarvātma bhāva), it is the experience of the Universal Self, the Bliss of *brahman*. The terms "everything" and "Universal" include the triad - jagat, jīvā, and Iśvara. The notion of jagat engenders the notion of a jīvā, and the notion of a jīvā engenders the notion of Iśvara. Therefore, if the notion of jagat disappears, the remaining two notions will also disappear. This disappearance of the world, the individual, and Iśvara of Advaita is not like the "nothingness" of the materialists nor the "emptiness" of the Buddhists. All though the three entities (jīvā, jagat, Iśvara) are unreal and have no separate existence of their own, as Consciousness, they are Real. When they dissolve in ātmā, what remains is ātmā alone. This experience of Oneness is sarvātmabhāva.

The one who attains such a Unified Vision is liberated. He is a jīvānmukta. He is not yet a videhamukta because he still has a body. Complete liberation (videhamukti) is possible when prārabdha karma is fully exhausted and the body dies. Until then, the jīvānmukta continues to live. Instead of wasting his life on body-maintenance (food, bath, etc.), he dedicates his life to the upliftment of sincere seekers who have a burning desire for Self-Knowledge and liberation. The Self-Realized one transmits his knowledge and experience of the Self to others through his speech and writings. This is the meaning of the word *saṅkīrtana* in verse ten. Shankara lists *saṅkīrtana* as the fourth step in the practice, following śravaṇa, manana, and nididhyāsana.

Such a realized being is a jīvānmukta, a fully Accomplished One. Since he is completely identified with the Supreme Self, he has all the powers of the Supreme Self, the most important of them being expansiveness - the ability to see everything everywhere as the expansion (vibhūti) of his own Self. With a Self that is unrestrained and all-pervading, a jīvānmukta, like Iśvara, can use his māyā śakti to manifest anything. He automatically gets the power of command over the different worlds and the beings in those worlds. He also acquires all the yogic powers- anima, garima, laguma, etc., like the ones Lord Hanuman displayed in Ramayana.

The jīvānmukta, however, does not display his powers for trivial reasons. Unlike an ordinary yogi who exhibits his powers to impress others, a jīvānmukta does not have a wavering mind. He has no desire to exhibit his powers, since he perceives everything as the Supreme Self. When everything is *brahman*, and there is nobody or nothing inside or outside of *brahman*, who is there to exhibit and to whom? Only because a jīvānmukta does not have any desires, he is able to see everything as *brahman*. If he happens to display his powers occasionally, it is only in response to particular needs of the people around him or to accomplish a particular task that is prompted by the Divine Will. He is simply a means through which things manifest. Even when his powers are operating, like the people around him, he too simply stands and watches his performance like a spectator. Hence, he is a *siddha purusha*, the Accomplished One.

Conclusion

The *Hymn to Lord Dakṣiṇāmūrti* now comes to an end. The problem, the solution, and the outcome have been clearly explained by Shankara. The outcome sarvātmabhāva, the experience of the Self in All, is within our reach because it is our very nature. It is present in the beginning (before birth), in the middle (while living), and in the end (after death). Unfortunately, we forget this truth and search for it, like searching elsewhere for the gold chain that has been hanging on our own neck the whole time. Wherever we search for it, we will not find it. Only when we feel our neck and touch the gold chain, we will realize that it has been with us all the time. Similar effort is required for us to realize that our very own Self is the Universal Self.

Caught in the vicious cycle of saṃsāra, we have forgotten that the world we see is only an appearance of the Universal Self. We have unnecessarily made the world a complex problem. We have to remember what we have forgotten. Shankara calls this remembrance pratyabhigna. A satguru, a true teacher, can facilitate such an experience of pratyabhigna in the student. Shankara is such a teacher. Having realized the Self, he shares his experience with seekers like us.

Through the study of this hymn, we have circumambulated Lord Dakṣiṇāmūrti, the Supreme Self who assumes the form of a Guru to teach His disciples. We have started with the Self and have ended with the Self. That is why I titled my commentary *Dakṣiṇāmūrti Pradakṣiṇa* (Circumambulation of Lord Dakṣiṇāmūrti). He is the

Guru and the Self. After performing a Hindu ritual, the worshipper offers ātmā pradakṣiṇa. He circumambulates around himself three times as an offering to the Self. The self he offers is not the body, life-force, senses, intellect, or ego. It is the innermost Self (pratyagātmā), the Consciousness that is a silent witness to every action of the body and mind. It is that Self that we worship. It is the Supreme Self, which manifests as jīvā, jagat, and Iśvara. The circumambulation of Dakṣiṇāmūrti, therefore, is the circumambulation of our own Self, which is not different from the Universal Self. This experience of the Universal Self is the great fruit that Shankara promises as a result of sincere effort in the form of śravaṇa, manana, and nididhyāsana.

Sages compare saṃsāra to a tree and mokṣa (liberation) to its fruit. A tree grows from a seed and eventually bears fruit. If we cut open the fruit, we will find the seed once again. Therefore, in the beginning and in the end there is the seed. In the middle, there is its expansion from seed to tree. Therefore, it is the same substance that appears in different forms in different stages. This hymn reveals this truth. It starts with the form of Dakṣiṇāmūrti and ends with It. To be more precise, it starts with a form and ends with the formless. Whatever we perceive as names and forms are essentially a manifestation of the formless Consciousness. Forms are an appearance, a decoration. Like a king who continues to be a king whether he wears a crown or not, Consciousness is ever present, with or without a form.

In this hymn, Lord Dakṣiṇāmūrti, the Supreme Consciousness, assumes the form of a teacher to teach His disciples the truth about the formless *brahman*. His teaching is in silence. His face is resplendent with Knowledge. His body shines covered in sacred ash. A luminous crescent moon adorns His head. In one of his hands, he holds a string of alphabets. He holds the musical instrument veena and a book in two other hands. His fourth hand is held in jñāna mudra. Seated in the position of a teacher, with a radiant and tranquil face, the Lord sits majestically and teaches the disciples seated around Him. May the Lord bestow His Grace on us at all times.

Not only is He Lord Dakṣiṇāmūrti (the Supreme Self), He is also Iśvara, the Creator. As Dakṣiṇāmūrti, He is omniscient. As Iśvara, He is omnipotent and omnipresent. He knows the suffering of the beings in the world and shows them ways to transcend it. His beautiful countenance fills the hearts of devotees who worship Him as their personal god with love and reverence. Many such personal gods can be found in any temple.

Personal gods with attributes belong to the relative world, not to the formless Absolute Reality. The Absolute alone can liberate us from bondage. As sincere seekers, our goal is to experience the formless Absolute reality. That is the only way we can break the bondage of saṃsāra. Forms and attributes are only an appearance of that formless creative power (māyā śakti) of *brahman*. They are merely symbols that point to the formless Reality.

According to mythology, Lord Shiva burned the demigod kāma to ashes and smeared the ashes on His body. There is a deep symbolism attached to this story. Kāma is desire for worldly pleasures. Desires are the result of our attachment to the world and the wrong notion that we are separate individuals. This attachment to the world and the feeling of separateness is due to ignorance (avidya). When Knowledge of the Self arises, desires and misconceptions about the world and the Self disappear. This is the meaning of the phrase "burning of kāma" - the annihilation of all desires and the transformation of the individual into a desire-free Self. Desire leads to action. When desire and action to satisfy the desire end, what remains is pure Knowledge or Consciousness.

The radiant presence of Lord Dakṣiṇāmūrti symbolizes this Pure Consciousness. When all desires are burned to ashes with Self Knowledge, Self alone shines. Reality is ever serene because It is the intrinsic nature of the Supreme Self. The individual consciousness is finite and fragmented. The goal of the seeker is to transcend his finitude and attain the Infinitude of the Supreme Self. Self-Knowledge is the only means to attain that goal.

Lord Dakṣiṇāmūrti is described as wearing a crescent moon on his head. The moon represents the mind, thoughts, perceptions, and feelings that are engendered by the world. As long as the mind is trapped in vritti-s, it operates as a separate self. The mind must transcend thoughts and become still. Only then it is possible for the individual Consciousness to merge in the Supreme Consciousness. This unification is yoga.

Surrounded by Sage Vashista, Sage Vāmadeva, and others, seated in the position of a teacher, Lord Dakṣiṇāmūrti silently transmits the most profound and sublime Knowledge of the Self to His disciples, who in turn transmit this Knowledge to their disciples.

To fully abide in the Self at all times, one must experience everything as the Self. This is sarvātma bhāva. Such an experience of Oneness is samādhi. Complete abidance in Lord Dakṣiṇāmūrti, the Formless, Immutable, Infinite Consciousness, will culminate in such an experience. Entering the temple of Lord Dakṣiṇāmūrti is to attain sarvātmābhāva.

www.ingramcontent.com/pod-product-compliance
Lightning Source LLC
LaVergne TN
LVHW041210150826
845673LV00001B/343

9798893222661